OUTGUNNED!

OUTGUNNED!

TRUE STORIES
of Citizens Who
Stood Up to Outlaws—
And Won

Robert A. Waters
and
John T. Waters, Jr.

Cumberland House
Nashville, Tennessee

Published by
Cumberland House Publishing, Inc.
431 Harding Industrial Drive
Nashville, TN 37211-3160

Cover design: Gore Studio, Inc.
Text design: John Mitchell

Library of Congress Cataloging-in-Publication Data
Waters, Robert A., 1944–
 Outgunned! : true stories of citizens who stood up to outlaws, and won / Robert A. Waters and John T. Waters, Jr.
    p. cm.
Includes bibliographical references.
ISBN 1-58182-386-X (pbk. : alk. paper)
 1. Victims of crimes—United States—History. 2. Vigilantes—United States—History.
 3. Vigilance committees—United States—History. 4. Outlaws—United States—History.
 I. Waters, John T. II. Title.
HV6250.3.U5W38 2004
362.88'092'273—dc22
                          2004007752

Printed in the United States of America
1 2 3 4 5 6 7—09 08 07 06 05 04

To our father, John T. Waters

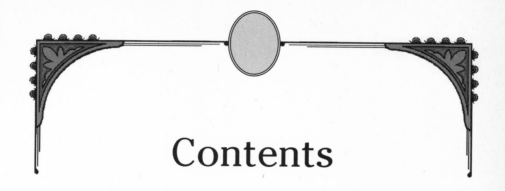

Contents

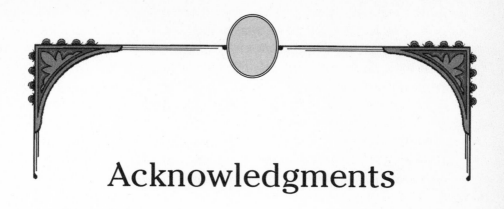

Acknowledgments

Thanks to Publisher Ron Pitkin and Editor John Mitchell for making this book a reality.

JOHN T. WATERS, JR.: I offer my warm thanks to the many generous people who found time to help me write this book.

Dannie Brown, a veteran law enforcement officer, advised me on certain esoteric facts. Charles Fuhs, a historian without a degree, supplied me with tidbits about the Old West which spurred me to dig deeper in my research. And to my genial friend Tess Bowers, who photographed me and cheered me through this endeavor, I owe a great debt.

And a special word of thanks is reserved for those who put up with me the longest. For my friends Gary Pascale, Alice Hodgkins, and Major Chris Flanagan, no praise is enough.

Finally, to my coworker and special friend—Lien Kim Williams Swab—nothing needs saying.

Robert A. Waters: I want to thank Marilyn, my long-suffering wife of thirty-one years, for her encouragement during the writing of this book.

My two children, Sim and LeAnn, always provide kind words for Dad's "hobby."

To my brother Zack and my sister Kim, thanks for being there.

To my longtime friends Fran, Dot, and Glenn Moore, I appreciate our time together and your constant encouragement.

Several individuals went above and beyond to provide information to a stranger. Frank Kennett, professor at University of Wisconsin–Stout and President of the Dunn County Historical Society, sent volumes of information about the Stout State Bank robbery. Thanks for taking the time to help a researcher you've never met. I'm also grateful to Mary Jane Nelson of the Johnston County Historical Society.

Marilyn Smith and Daphne Haworth of the Boone County Historical & Railroad Society and the Boone County Heritage Museum were very helpful. Thanks. Jeanette Haley, curator of the Lincoln County Historical Society, was gracious in sending information about the failed bank robberies at Stroud, Oklahoma. I appreciate your time and help.

The staff at the Oklahoma Historical Society was always helpful in copying newspaper articles and forwarding them in record time.

Ardith Douglas, curator of the White River Museum and Rio Blanco County Historical Society in Meeker, Colorado, provided much-needed information.

Catherine Paula Curry, granddaughter of Paul Curry, sent information about the life of her grandfather.

Finally, as always, I am grateful for the lasting friendship of the members of the Central Church of Christ in Ocala, Florida.

A town that won't defend itself deserves no help.
— Martin, from the movie *High Noon*

A gun is a tool like any other, as good or as bad as the man who uses it.
— Shane, from the movie *Shane*

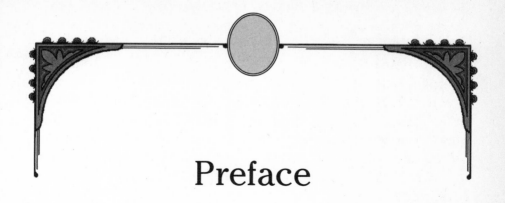

Preface

At three o'clock on the afternoon of October 13, 1896, two men entered the Bank of Meeker, Colorado. They were George Law and "Kid" Pierce, both members of Butch Cassidy's Wild Bunch. Law walked up to David Smith, a cashier, and fired a warning shot past his head. When the startled Smith didn't immediately raise his hands, Law fired again. He then produced a sugar sack and motioned for Smith to fill it.

The gunshots alerted townspeople to the robbery in progress. Within minutes, more than a dozen citizens armed with rifles, shotguns, and pistols had formed a perimeter around the bank.

Outside, Jim Shirley, the robbers' lookout, became frustrated with the gathering crowd, so he shot W. H. Smith, killing him.

Moments later, Law and Pierce came out of the bank, marching several hostages in front of them. With Shirley providing covering fire, the outlaws made their way down the street to their horses.

But as Shirley and Law attempted to untie their mounts, one of their hostages broke away. Pierce opened fire at the fleeing man, causing the other captives to scatter. This gave the armed citizens the chance they were waiting for. A volley of gunfire erupted from the edges of the streets. Shirley and Pierce went down, mortally wounded. Law dropped the stolen sack of money and fled on foot toward the outskirts of town. A second fusillade stopped him cold. Within minutes, all three outlaws were dead.

On the morning of October 20, 1931, Winfield Kern, owner of a restaurant in Menomonie, Wisconsin, saw a large black Lincoln town car pull to the curb in front of the Kraft State Bank. His curiosity turned to alarm when three suspicious-looking men got out of the expensive vehicle and went inside, leaving a fourth man, later identified as a small-time gangster named Frank Webber, standing guard by the car.

Inside the bank, the trio brandished weapons and forced patrons onto the floor as they retrieved $90,000 in cash and securities from the safe. During the confusion, a bank guard pressed the alarm button. With the shrill horn blaring in the cold morning air, everyone in town quickly became aware that the bank was being robbed.

As citizens, many of them carrying firearms, began to congregate, Webber grew nervous. He pulled a machine gun from the car and strafed the nearby storefronts, but he was unable to quell the growing crowd. A contemporary account of the robbery states that "the bank's door flew open and the robbers exited using young James Kraft and a very frightened Mrs. A. W. Schafer as hostages and shields. Mrs. Schafer stumbled and fell to the sidewalk, which probably saved her life because the frantic men did not stop to pick her up as they rushed to the waiting getaway car."

Winfield Kern, Ed Grutt (a clerk in the Farmer's Store), and other citizens began a withering fire at the outlaws. Webber took a bullet in the eye, and Charles Preston Harmon, another of the robbers, was hit in the neck, but the gangsters managed to run the gauntlet of gunfire and make it to their car. Still holding the unlucky Kraft as a hostage, they roared away.

Several citizens, along with the Dunn County sheriff, jumped into their cars and began pursuing the bandits.

Webber, screaming from the pain of his wounds, died a few minutes into the chase and was dumped along the roadside. Harmon died later. As an act of revenge, the two remaining robbers shot and killed James Kraft and threw his body from the car.

The two surviving bandits made good their escape, but they were captured a few months later and sentenced to long prison terms in the federal penitentiary at Leavenworth, Kansas. It turned out that they were members of the Keating Gang, which had connections to George "Machine Gun" Kelly and Alvin "Creepy" Karpis.

Many thousands of books have been written about the bloody deeds of Wild West outlaws and Prohibition-era gangsters.

Romance and legend have fogged reality and, in many cases, made heroes of these bandits and murderers. Their names are etched in our collective psyche: Billy the Kid, Jesse James, Butch Cassidy and the Sundance Kid, Cole Younger, the Daltons, Belle Starr, and lesser-known outlaws such as Black Jack Ketchum, the Cherokee Kid, and hundreds more. Even eighty years after their heyday, gangsters like John Dillinger, Bonnie and Clyde, Pretty Boy Floyd, the Barkers, Bugs Moran, Machine Gun Kelly, and Baby Face Nelson remain household names.

Numerous books have also been written about the lawmen who pursued the desperados. Sheriff Pat Garrett, Wyatt Earp, the Pinkertons, the Texas Rangers, and Heck Thomas were among those who, at least in the public's imagination, fought for law and order. (Garrett, Earp, and many other lawmen in the Old West were borderline criminals themselves—but that's another story.) Then there was J. Edgar Hoover, who made it his mission to go after the Prohibition-era gangsters.

But from the very beginning, other forces were at work in the fight against crime. The decent, unsung citizens who populated the towns and villages of America did as much to bring law and order to the nation as the lawmen, judges, and jailers. Wherever they settled, they established churches and schools. They farmed small plots or raised cattle on the open range. They were bankers, store owners, craftsmen, laborers, entrepreneurs, and ministers.

They were also the people on whom the outlaws preyed.

As the United States expanded westward, many thousands of people followed. They came from the East, the South, the Midwest, and from almost every other country on earth. The Old West was a true melting pot of races, nationalities, and religions. Some settlers came to work the mines—gold, silver, copper, and lead were there for the taking if one could locate a vein and was willing to do the back-breaking work to extract the precious ore. Others moved west to sell goods to the new settlers, or to squat on "free" homesteads, or to work the railroads, or to pan for gold. Most believed they could strike it rich—and some did.

In short, these men and women, each in his or her own way, were seeking opportunity.

Criminals and malcontents followed in their wake like sharks. They sought to steal the hard-earned wealth of those willing to work. Though there were numerous sociological factors involved in the making of the western outlaw and the latter-day gangster, the fact is that most craved the good life but were unwilling to do the labor required to achieve it. They often used the excuse that they were "fighting against evil capitalists who exploited the working man." In many cases, the poor *were* exploited, but the bandits who robbed and murdered were far worse than the capitalists they sought to blame.

At least the capitalists would work for their money.

While robbers occasionally gave money to the poor like the Robin Hoods they pretended to be, the real reason they did so was to buy the friendship of those who could help them avoid capture. And a strong populist sentiment in middle America sometimes made heroes of those who "stole from the rich and gave to the poor."

The ploy worked, at least to a degree. Outlaws often had family and friends who were willing to hide them and to throw pursuing lawmen off their trail.

But there were others who had no truck with the criminals.

In town after town, as bandits attempted to rob banks or businesses, they were set upon by armed citizens. In fact, smart bandits planned for citizen intervention. Before robbing a bank in Caney, Kansas, Henry Starr wrote in his autobiography that "we planned to conceal our rifles about two miles from town and felt that we would be able to do the bank and get to the street before the alarm was given, then a few more seconds would bring us to our horses, and if there was any shooting, we could give a pretty fair account with our pistols."

Starr's book, *Thrilling Events, Life of Henry Starr*, provides a disquieting insight into the mind of the western outlaw. Born in the Indian Territory near what is now Fort Gibson, Oklahoma, Starr was handsome, charming, courageous, daring, and innovative in planning his criminal activities. He was also addicted to crime and had no conscience. In the book *Henry Starr: The Last of the Real Bad Men*, Glenn Shirley writes:

> Three times [Starr] was to know the contentment of respectability, and was to produce a motion picture, *A Debtor to the Law*—his testament to the world that crime does not pay. But those who knew him best never believed he ever really reformed. He simply enjoyed raiding. He would laugh inwardly until he could hardly control himself at the enormous fright of his banker victims when he and his men would step in and take charge of all the loose currency . . .

17

In *Thrilling Events*, Starr blames everyone but himself for his criminal lifestyle. When, as a teenager, he was arrested for hauling illegal whiskey into the Indian Territory, he claimed he didn't know the whiskey was in the wagon. When he was arrested for stealing horses, he writes that he had "borrowed" the horse from a friend. When he shot and killed former Deputy U.S. Marshal Floyd Wilson in cold blood, he claimed it was self-defense. As for robbing banks—well, the greedy bankers deserved it.

To many, it seemed like poetic justice when the outlaw who "robbed more banks than any man in history" died at the hands of an armed banker while attempting a holdup in Harrison, Arkansas.

Outgunned! cuts through the mist of legend and describes true stories of armed citizens who went up against outlaws and gangsters—and won.

Some stories would be humorous if they weren't so tragic. Take the case of the hoodlum wannabe who tried to rob a Texas bank two days before Christmas while wearing, of all things, a Santa Claus outfit. But as Marshall Ratliff and his gang exited the bank with a bag full of cash, they were shot by the townspeople.

While some of the incidents related here have become part of American lore, such as the James Gang's attempt to rob a bank in Northfield, Minnesota, and the Dalton Gang's fiasco in Coffeyville, Kansas, most are little-known vignettes of history, such as the story of the only man ever executed in the state of Michigan.

When Anthony Chebatoris and his partner tried to rob the Chemical State Savings Bank in Midland, Michigan, on July 8, 1938, they were shot by an armed dentist who kept a hunting rifle in his office—but not before they had killed an innocent passerby.

Unlike his partner, Chebatoris survived the shootout and was sentenced to death by a federal judge (because the bank was a depository for federally insured money).

Despite Michigan's long-standing statute outlawing capital punishment, the federal government insisted that the criminal be executed in the state in which he committed his crimes. In the days leading up to the execution, Michigan's governor lodged a series of protests with President Franklin Delano Roosevelt. But all was in vain. On July 8, 1938, Chebatoris went to the gallows.

In still another case, on November 22, 1932, George T. Birdwell, one of Pretty Boy Floyd's henchmen, and two accomplices attempted to rob the Farmers & Merchants Bank in the all-black town of Boley, Oklahoma. Of all the days of the year, they picked the first day of hunting season—which assured that plenty of guns would be available to the local citizenry. All three robbers (two white and one black) were quickly dispatched.

Then there's the bizarre story of Black Jack Ketchum, a Texas train robber and murderer. As Ketchum attempted his last heist, the conductor grabbed a shotgun and blasted the bandit's right arm off. Ketchum, unable to mount his horse and escape, was captured the following day by a posse. He was tried for several cold-blooded killings and sentenced to hang. As if that weren't bad enough, the hangman was an amateur who tied the noose so tight that when Ketchum dropped through the trap door in the scaffold's floor, his head was severed from his body. A local doctor sewed it back on before the bandit was buried.

The stories in *Outgunned!* tell a different story than the standard folklore about the bandits and gangsters who rode the outlaw trail. The book describes them as they really were—cutthroat thugs who would not hesitate to murder so that they could enjoy the good life without working for it.

The book also tells of many everyday citizens who fought back, who helped bring law and order to the towns and cities of the growing nation, and who changed America for the better.

OUTGUNNED!

The Hog Gun

A hog gun, and a kid, too. I wouldn't have minded
it so much if a man had shot me.
— Henry Starr, notorious bank robber, after
being gunned down by teenager Paul Curry

March 27, 1915, was a Saturday. It was nine o'clock in the
morning when gunfire erupted on the normally peaceful streets of Stroud, Oklahoma.

Seventeen-year-old Paul Curry was in his back yard
nearby. Looking up when he heard the noise, he was
amazed to see three men with guns exit the Stroud State
Bank, marching a group of hostages in front of them.

By now, bursts of gunfire were sounding every few seconds. Townspeople, many of them armed, had taken refuge
behind wagons, railings, or anything else they could find and
were pouring fire at the robbers. The outlaws, trying to control their captives, walked quickly down East Third Street,
occasionally turning to shoot into the pursuing crowd.

Rows of businesses lined both sides of East Third Street
as it approached the intersection with South Fourth

Avenue, which led to the stockyard south of town. At the junction of those two streets stood the First National Bank, a brick structure that was by far Stroud's largest and most impressive building, with leaded-glass windows and a high circular turret overlooking the town.

As he watched the events unfold, Paul Curry decided he had to help his friends. Staying out of the line of fire, he ran about a hundred yards to his father's grocery store directly across from the First National. Ducking inside, he grabbed a .30-30 Winchester rifle. The gun had been sawed off, leaving about an inch of the barrel protruding above the forestock. The gun had a specific purpose: It was used for killing hogs when they were ready to be butchered. The teenager thumbed several rounds into the chamber, then raced back outside.

Curry noticed that most of the townspeople were too far away from the bandits to hit anyone. Their shots kicked up dust but never came close to the outlaws. The youngster calculated the path of the robbers and decided to cut them off. According to Glenn Shirley, author of *Henry Starr, Last of the Real Bad Men*, "Curry ran to the rear of the store,

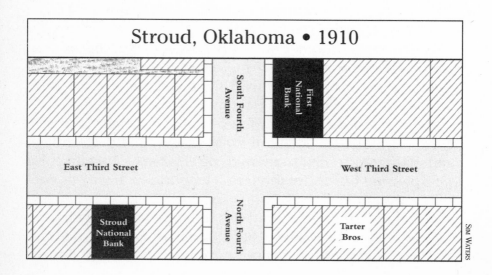

Stroud, Oklahoma • 1910

South Fourth Avenue

First National Bank

East Third Street

West Third Street

North Fourth Avenue

Stroud National Bank

Tarter Bros.

Sim Waters

taking a position behind two salt barrels." Now he had a clear view of South Fourth Street, which is where the robbers seemed to be headed. His position also allowed the teenager to peer into the alley directly across the street. It was the same alley that Henry Starr would use as he attempted to escape.

Curry was familiar with guns. He helped his father slaughter hogs, and he was an avid hunter. He cradled the hog gun in both hands and waited.

As the bandits and their hostages approached the First National, a second group of men, also with captives in tow, exited from the bank's rear door and entered the alley. As the two groups of gunmen joined forces, it suddenly occurred to Curry that they were a gang of crooks trying to pull a double bank robbery—just like the Daltons had tried, but failed, to do.

His intuition was right. An article in *The Daily Oklahoman* on April 1, 1915, stated, "The Starr gang of desperados rode into town and held up the First National Bank, of Stroud, and secured $4,000. Then the Stroud National Bank was held up and $1,700 taken. . . ." Actually, both banks were robbed simultaneously by two groups of three gunmen, while one man waited near the stockyard holding their getaway horses.

As the robbers prodded their captives down South Fourth, Curry recognized several prominent citizens among the hostages as well as J. B. Charles Jr., a bookkeeper at the Stroud State Bank, and one J. M. Reed.

The robbers were directly in front of him, maybe twenty feet away, when he noticed Stroud State Bank Vice President Samuel Lee Patrick. A tall, dark outlaw held a rifle against Patrick's back, forcing the frightened man to walk ahead of him. Because of his bearing, Curry guessed that this man was the gang's leader.

Just then, Charles Guild, a horse buyer, appeared in the alley behind the teenager. He held a double-barreled shotgun but never got the chance to fire it as the outlaw leader pushed Patrick out of the way and snapped off a shot at Guild. The bullet singed his vest, sending the horse buyer scurrying for cover.

This gave Curry the chance he needed. The other members of the gang had rushed ahead and were running toward their getaway horses. As soon as the outlaw leader pushed Patrick out of the way, Curry aimed his rifle and fired.

"The heavy slug struck [Starr] in the left thigh," wrote Shirley, "shattering the leg bone and knocking him down. Temporarily paralyzed about the waist, he tried to return the fire."

"Lay down your gun or I'll kill you!" Curry shouted, aiming his own weapon at the outlaw's head.

Starr hesitated, then tossed the rifle a few feet away.

Curry noticed that the man's leg was splayed at an awkward angle and that blood soaked the bandit's trousers.

As other citizens swarmed into the street to cover the downed outlaw, Curry made his way toward the stockyard.

Several bandits had already gotten there and quickly retrieved their mounts, and were riding away, stopping long enough to fire a few volleys at the townspeople.

One outlaw, however, was walking straight toward Curry. Still holding two bank employees hostage, the man seemed confused as he led a skittish horse by the reins. Curry suddenly realized that the bandit wasn't confused at all—he was coming back to pick up the wounded robber.

The teenager waited until he had an open shot and then fired.

The outlaw staggered backward and almost fell. Recovering, he placed a pistol in the face of one of the captives and ordered the man to help him up on his horse. With the help of a second hostage, the robber climbed onto the back of his mount.

Curry watched the bandit swaying in the saddle as he rode away.

The boy was in shock as he thought about what he'd done. Walking back down Fourth Avenue toward the center of town, he noticed that his hands were trembling.

He saw several townspeople carrying the wounded robber toward the doctor's office.

"You know who this is?" someone asked.

Curry shook his head.

"Henry Starr! You shot Henry Starr!"

"You sure?" Curry asked in disbelief, but the man already had moved on.

Crowds were whooping in the streets. It sounded like Independence Day. The teenager watched as Sheriff George Arnold and Deputy Hi Frisbie gathered citizens for a posse. Within minutes, the lawmen had commandeered a Model T Ford, and Curry watched them putter out of town, followed by the rest of the posse riding horses.

A wagon pulled up. It was Curry's brother. "Come on," the breathless boy shouted. Paul climbed into the wagon and it careened away, following the Model T as best it could.

Henry Starr once boasted that he'd robbed more banks than any man in history.

Part Cherokee, he was born in 1873 and raised near Fort Gibson, in the Indian Territory. At seventeen, he was convicted of selling illegal whiskey to the Indians and fined $100. A year later, he was arrested for horse theft. When a friend posted his bail, Starr immediately jumped bond. An arrest warrant was issued. Several robberies of local general stores were blamed on Starr, and soon he was being chased by the Indian Police.

On December 13, 1892, Floyd Wilson, a former deputy U.S. marshal who was working as a private detective, tried to arrest Starr. In the ensuing gunfight, the lawman was hit and fell to the ground. As Wilson lay helpless, Starr walked up, placed his rifle barrel directly against the detective's chest, and fired.

Before he'd turned twenty, Henry Starr was wanted for murder.

The following year, while still on the run for the killing of Wilson, Starr and an accomplice robbed several railroad depots. Their total take was only a few hundred dollars, so they decided to go after bigger paydays.

On December 28, 1893, Starr held up the Caney Valley Bank in Caney, Kansas, getting away with $4,900.

Now the outlaw had found his calling.

A few weeks later, he and his gang robbed the People's Bank in Bentonville, Arkansas, this time gathering more than $11,000.

In 1894, Starr was captured and convicted of Wilson's murder, and Judge Isaac Parker sentenced him to hang. Starr's lawyer appealed the case to the U.S. Supreme Court, and the justices overturned his conviction, citing the "prejudicial" nature of Parker's Court. Starr was granted a new trial and was promptly found guilty. But once again, the Supreme Court remanded the case and ordered another trial.

After a series of legal maneuvers, the outlaw pled guilty to manslaughter and seven counts of armed robbery and was facing a fifteen-year term in a federal prison.

It was during his incarceration in the Fort Smith jail while awaiting sentencing that Starr committed an act of heroism that would later get him pardoned.

Dozens of convicted murderers were housed in the jail. Like Starr, they were awaiting sentencing and would either face the gallows or be transferred to a federal penitentiary. One was a vicious killer named Crawford Goldsby, also known as Cherokee Bill, who had murdered five men and shot several more who managed to survive. Considered incorrigible and uncontrollable by his jailers, he had a hair-trigger temper that caused many of the other outlaws to stay as far away from him as they could.

It wasn't long before Cherokee Bill began plotting a jailbreak. Someone smuggled a revolver into the jail for him, and on July 26, 1895, Cherokee Bill and another convicted murderer named George Pearce tried to escape. During the attempt, Bill shot and killed Lawrence Keating, a guard. Then pair then rushed from their cells and fled down the hall toward the door.

Other guards were quickly summoned and blocked the escape route. A gun battle ensued, and Bill was forced back down the hall and into his cell. Because of Bill's accuracy with a pistol, guards were unable to get close enough to shoot him, and the situation turned into a stalemate. Bill would fire at anything that moved, all the while emitting a high-pitched "Indian death gobble." He even shot at guards who attempted to move Keating's body.

After a standoff of several hours, Henry Starr sent word to the warden that he, being friends with Cherokee Bill, could get the murderer to give up his gun. Starr's only request was that the guards not kill the bloodthirsty outlaw.

The warden had no alternative but to agree. Starr walked down the narrow passage to Cherokee Bill's cell, was allowed to enter, and after a few minutes walked out holding Bill's gun. The guards then converged on the cell and dragged Bill out. It was only due to the warden's intervention that Bill and Pearce weren't lynched then and there by prison guards. (Cherokee Bill cheated the rope for only a short time—he was hanged on March 17, 1896. When asked if he had any last words, the outlaw is said to have responded, "I came here to die, not to make a speech.")

In 1898, while awaiting sentencing in the Fort Smith jail, Starr, with the help of a local reporter, began writing his memoirs. The outlaw, already notorious throughout the Indian Territory, would work on his book off and on for many years, and it would be published in 1914 under the title *Thrilling Events, Life of Henry Starr*.

After serving several years of his sentence, Starr got a break. The outlaw, now an inmate at the federal penitentiary in Columbus, Ohio, learned that President Theodore Roosevelt was looking into his case. Roosevelt had heard of Starr's heroic action in disarming Cherokee Bill, and, impressed by his courage, was considering a full and complete pardon for the outlaw. Starr's mother, hearing this, set upon the president like a wildcat on a rabbit, relentlessly writing long and profuse letters relating how her son had mended his ways.

In 1902, Starr was released from prison with a presidential pardon. It didn't take the outlaw long to make Roosevelt regret his decision.

Starr went to work at a restaurant in Tulsa. He married and had a son he named Theodore Roosevelt Starr. On the surface he seemed to have settled down.

But the call of the outlaw trail was too much. He and a former gang member, Kid Wilson, robbed a bank in Tyro, Kansas. A posse quickly formed and chased the bandits back into the Indian Territory. By now, rewards for Starr (who had been recognized while robbing the bank) had reached nearly $2,500 "dead or alive."

Starr and Wilson eventually made their way to Colorado, robbing a bank in Amity along the way. With the law hot on their trail, they split up, and Starr hid out in Arizona. It was there, in the village of Bosque, that he was captured again.

Starr was extradited back to Colorado. He was tried and convicted of robbing the Amity bank and sentenced to seven to twenty-five years. He was a model prisoner, as always. It was during this time, in July 1914, that the outlaw's autobiography was published.

The parole board had read the galleys sometime before publication and, in what must be one of the most ill-advised decisions ever made by such a body, decided that Starr was a good candidate for release. It's hard to determine what they saw in the book that would make them consider the outlaw a reformed man. In his memoirs, Starr never takes the blame for any of his actions. He implies that society is at fault, particularly his many tormentors—judges, lawmen, and jailers.

The book is a blatant attempt to romanticize his own legend and to justify his actions. Starr offers numerous examples of uncritical self-justification. To quote one instance, when the warden of the Lamar, Colorado, jail turned away several friends who had come to visit Starr, he wrote, "It didn't make any difference what I had done, they had no right to put me in solitary confinement before I had a trial; not apt to increase a man's respect for law and order nor that intangible thing they call society."

The underlying message in Starr's memoirs is that he had nothing but contempt for the law. This is also illustrated by his unwillingness to take any responsibility for his actions, and his apparent lack of remorse for those he hurt.

Another excerpt describes his attitude toward work. Before his incarceration in the federal prison in Ohio, Starr's lawyer worked out what was, for those times, an unusual agreement. Starr writes, "My sentence read that no part of it should be spent at hard labor, and my work (inside the prison] was piece-meal and easy."

In more than one passage, he romanticizes the bank robber. "There's a sort of hypnotism," he wrote, "about a man or a bunch of men who come coolly into a town in the middle of the day, walk up the main street, rob a bank, and walk out again, doing just enough shooting to prove that they can hit anything. The very daring of it puts a spell on people, paralyzes them with surprise and awe. Before they recover, the bandits are gone."

In spite of his obvious hatred of law-abiding society, the bank robber was paroled, with the stipulation that he remain in Colorado.

Starr opened a restaurant in the town of Holly but soon became intimate with the wife of a local businessman.

Amid a burgeoning scandal, the lovers fled. This violated his parole, and Starr once again was a wanted man.

Now an orgy of bank robberies began, the likes of which the United States had never before seen. Fourteen banks in

Oklahoma were robbed within a four-month stretch. Howls from bankers and the legislature once again set the full force of the law on Starr's trail.

"These flagrant and successful daylight depredations left the state agape," writes Shirley. "The Southwest was shocked. Insurance companies threatened to cancel bank policies, and the harassed Oklahoma legislature, for the first time in its history, moved swiftly to pass a hurriedly drawn 'bank-robber bill,' appropriating $15,000 for the capture or death of 'highwaymen and safe-blowers' and empowering the chief executive to place a price on the heads of bandits not to exceed $1,000 in any one case."

Starr was the first bandit to have the bounty placed on his head. But it seemed no one could catch him—he was always a step ahead of his pursuers.

Then, on Saturday, March 27, 1915, Starr and six confederates rode into Stroud, Oklahoma.

Stroud was like many small western towns in 1915. It was primarily rural, but the appearance of motorcars and telephone lines were beginning to nudge the settlement into the modern age. Still, dirt streets became muddy when it rained and dusty when it was dry. Along Third Street (now Main Street), an assortment of businesses stood like an oasis for the farmers who came to town once a month.

Stroud had begun in 1898 as a "whiskey town." It was only one and a half miles from the Indian Territory, where spirits were illegal. But those with a thirst regularly left the Territory and made their way into the booming little settlement, frequenting its nine saloons or purchasing bootleg whiskey.

But by 1915, the town had cleaned itself up. No longer did the rough element walk its streets. With schools, churches, and legitimate businesses, Stroud had become a place where decent citizens could raise their children.

An hour after Starr had been captured, members of the posse located the second robber. Lewis Estes had been shot in the neck by Curry but had been able to mount his horse and ride away. A mile and a half from town, he could continue no longer. He was discovered propped against a tree. When the posse arrived, Estes held one hand up as a sign of surrender.

The robber joined Starr in the offices of Dr. John Evans.

When told that Estes had tried to return and pick him up, Starr stated that the bandit was a "good boy." He then informed the doctor that the gang had an agreement that if any of them were shot, the others would continue on. It was every man for himself, the outlaw said.

The doctor examined Starr and determined that the slug in his leg needed to be removed. It was said that he never flinched during the operation.

Starr asked the doctor to identify the man who had shot him. When informed that the gunman was a seventeen-year-old, he asked, "What did the kid shoot me with?"

"I'll be damned," Starr replied when he was told that the boy had used a hog rifle. "I don't mind getting shot. It had to happen sooner or later. But a kid with a hog gun—that hurts my pride."

Starr immediately set about ingratiating himself with anyone he thought could help him. He gave Dr. Evans his black horse, a thoroughbred that had become famous for outrunning many a posse. "He cost me five hundred dollars," Starr said. "But I won't be needing him any longer."

Lee Patrick, the bank president, marched over to confiscate a gold tie pin that Starr had stolen from him during the heist. The outlaw apologized for robbing his bank and holding him hostage. Patrick, who'd felt bullets whizzing about his face, snatched the tie pin from the bandit and left without speaking.

Outside, in the street below the office, citizens were gathering. While the conversation began as excited chatter about the outlaw gang and the attempted robberies, it soon turned ugly. People began to loudly proclaim their intention of stringing up the bandits.

In Dr. Evans's office, Starr could hear the threats. "Doc," he begged, "give me some poison. I don't mind dying, but I don't want to hang."

According to one source, he used the doctor's telephone to call the famous U.S. Deputy Marshal Bill Tilghman, who happened to be in nearby Oklahoma City. Starr pleaded with the lawman to come to Stroud and stop the citizens from lynching him.

Tilghman arrived the following day. He greeted Starr as if he were an old friend, and promised to make sure that the bandit got a fair trial.

By this time, Sheriff Arnold, Deputy Frisbie and a posse of local citizens were hot on the trail of the remaining robbers. In addition, county officials called out the militia. These armed citizens were instrumental in eventually capturing all the outlaws.

Using motorcars, they drove into the hills surrounding Stroud. They managed to keep the fugitives bottled up in groves of timber several miles from the city, and kept them from escaping into the Osage country. One by one, the bandits were run down and captured. Almost all of the money taken in the two robberies was recovered, much to bankers' relief.

Once the doctor had completed his work on Starr, the outlaw was transferred to the Lincoln County Jail in Chandler. As the other members of the gang were captured, they also were brought to the jail. Eventually, in return for a lenient sentence, Estes turned informer. His testimony ensured the conviction of all except one bandit, who was inexplicably acquitted.

Once again, Starr got seven to twenty-five years.

Paul Curry, the boy with the hog gun, was advised to apply for the $1,000 reward. He did so, stating that if he received the money he planned to use it for an education.

The Oklahoma governor put him off, however, stating that Starr would have to be convicted before Curry could get the reward money.

An article in *The Oklahoma Leader* described Curry's dilemma:

> Paul Curry, the . . . boy who shot and captured Henry Starr is being deluged with letters, with offers to go on the stage and to act in moving pictures. The boy is only a country youth with little education but he is bearing the praise and notoriety that have come to him very modestly. A Muskogee newspaperman wrote young Curry several days ago, asking for a photograph and information as to what the boy intended doing with the $1,000 reward for capturing Starr. Since [that time] young Curry has asked for the reward and learned that its payment depends upon Starr's conviction.
>
> It was probably just after he received this information that Paul penned the answer to the question of how it feels to get a thousand dollars for shooting a desperado. "Dear Sir: Excuse my hurrying but I have many letters to answer. As for pictures I have taken none as yet, I do not expect no thousand dollars. I don't think the Gov. has enough . . . money . . . although I would like to have it."

Curry was right. Once Starr was convicted, the governor claimed that he had no money to pay the reward, even though the legislature had granted the money in its "bank robber bill." According to relatives, the boy who shot Henry Starr never received a penny.

Paul Curry became everything Henry Starr was not. When World War I broke out, Curry joined the Army and

OUTGUNNED!

served in combat in France. He later attended Oklahoma A & M College (now Oklahoma State University) and obtained his teacher's certificate. Curry became a teacher and part-time farmer. He married and had four children. He lived an honorable life and was well respected in his community. Paul Curry died in 1952 while on the operating table to have an ulcer repaired.

As always, Henry Starr was a model prisoner. He quickly convinced his jailers that he had been framed. Within months of his incarceration, the chaplain at the Oklahoma State Prison began to proselytize for the outlaw's release. "This man has undoubtedly reformed," he was prone to telling anybody who would listen to him.

Others joined the chorus, including Streeter Speakman, the man who had prosecuted Starr. "Considering his aged and crippled condition, I believe he will bring his career as a bank robber to a close as soon as he regains his freedom. He is a man of unusual intelligence. He is not a low, depraved type of humanity, and is capable of making a good citizen."

Speakman, in referring to Starr's "crippled condition," acknowledged the permanent limp produced by Paul Curry's bullet.

To cap off the clamor for Starr's release, Kate Bernard, Oklahoma's Commissioner of Charities and Corrections, weighed in. Bernard held a firm belief that society formed criminals, that all men were good deep down, and that if they had the chance they would all go straight.

"I have studied men," she said, "until I know from the shape of their hands and head, the gait of their walk and the contour of their faces, much of their mode of life and the character of their thoughts . . . and Starr has made one of the sincerest efforts at reformation of all the 20,000 convicts I have known."

Those who questioned the sincerity of the outlaw's reform were ruthlessly silenced by Bernard's virulence. She

Photos Courtesy of Jeannette Haley and Lincoln County Historical Society

Henry Starr used this .35-caliber Remington semiautomatic rifle during his gang's disastrous raid on Stroud, Oklahoma. After the gunfight, in which Starr was wounded, the outlaw gave the weapon to Lee Patrick, one of the hostages, who in 1963 donated it to the Lincoln County Historical Society (inset).

was said to have considered it a personal affront when anyone dared suggest that Starr should serve his full sentence.

Her influence won the day.

Henry Starr, who had lived nearly his whole life as an outlaw, was paroled on March 15, 1919.

On that morning, he could have walked from the prison into a long, satisfying, and respectable life. He was lucky to be alive. In addition to being one of the few murderers to escape the noose of Isaac Parker, "the Hanging Judge," on two occasions, he also had escaped death after being shot during the Stroud robberies. Many men would have considered the risks and determined that crime doesn't pay.

But Henry Starr was different.

Inside his mind there danced visions of easy money, cowering bank tellers, and adrenaline-filled getaways leaving posses trailing behind like a gaggle of lame racehorses.

In a passage near the end of his book (which should have given the parole board pause), Starr details a bizarre rationale for committing his crimes:

A lot of people will be curious to know about certain things, so I'll ask and answer. What is your politics? Haven't any. Your religion? Same. Do you think you led a correct life? No, but it's as good as some others that are holding office. Do you think society is going to the dogs? No I don't; it never was away from them. Don't you feel that it's a great crime to take people's money? Yes, I know it's wrong, but I'm only a small thief, the lawyers take it all away from me, and still I go to the penitentiary. The big thieves never go to the pen, and besides, they keep what they steal. For that reason, I feel much abused.

Nothing could change the outlaw.

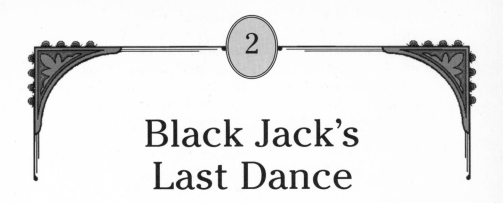

Black Jack's Last Dance

I'll die as I lived.

— Black Jack Ketchum, declining the offer of a priest
and requesting a fiddle so he could dance before being
hanged in Clayton, New Mexico

The old smoker chugged away from the depot at Trinity, in the New Mexico Territory, on August 16, 1897. It was already dark when the engine, mail car, passenger car, and caboose had stopped at the station. Owned by the Colorado & Southern Railway Company, the train was optimistically called the *Texas Fast Flyer*.

At around 11 p.m., as it rounded Twin Mountains, near Folsom, New Mexico, a lone figure crept into the engine's cab. The fireman was stoking the flames, and the engineer had his eye on the tracks ahead.

They never heard the man coming.

Thomas Edward "Black Jack" Ketchum was a notorious train robber who'd once hidden out with Butch Cassidy's gang. He entered the cab, pulled a pearl-handled Colt .45 revolver, and ordered the engineer to stop the train.

39

The *Flyer* jerked as it slowed, throwing passengers from their seats.

Ketchum's plan was to disconnect the express car and the two mail cars, then pull them about a mile up the track away from the remaining cars. This would have left the rest of the train and the passengers behind, leaving only the fireman, the engineer, and the express manager for him to contend with. He had left dynamite and supplies in a cave near Twin Mountains, about a mile from where he planned to stop the train.

But the outlaw had miscalculated. He forced the fireman to stop on a curve where there was "about a four-foot fill." This left the train in a pinched position making it impossible for the engineer and the fireman to uncouple the cars. Ketchum would have to deal with more people than he had anticipated.

Conductor Frank Harrington was in the passenger car when the train stopped. He immediately suspected a robbery, as he's been robbed twice before. Harrington picked up his double-barrel 10-gauge shotgun and cocked both hammers. With his rear brakeman following, he crept forward toward the baggage car.

As he entered, he stumbled over the mail clerk who'd been shot in the jaw. The clerk later died of his wounds.

The conductor pressed forward toward the locomotive's cab, where he heard Ketchum threatening to kill the engineer if he and the fireman didn't get the express car uncoupled.

Harrington opened the back door of the cab and nudged the twin muzzles of the shotgun through it.

Ketchum spotted the conductor as he stepped through the door. The outlaw snapped off a shot. A split-second later, Harrington fired a blast at Ketchum.

The outlaw's shot missed. But a heavy charge of No. 1 buckshot smashed into Ketchum's right arm. Harrington screamed for the engineer to get the train moving.

As the *Texas Fast Flyer* lurched into motion, Ketchum staggered backward to the window. He dove out and rolled down the steep grade. When he came to rest, he managed to grasp his revolver with his left hand. He rose and raced to his horses. He was bleeding profusely and the horses smelled the blood. They shied away from the outlaw, then bolted for the open prairie.

Ketchum, unable to catch any of the horses, moved away from the track. He fell to the ground after stumbling for about a hundred yards. From the darkness, he watched as the train's fires roared and the cars rumbled away.

Lying in the sand, Ketchum fainted from the pain and loss of blood.

Conductor Harrington, upon arriving at the next station, sent a telegram to the sheriff in Trinidad, Colorado, to form a posse and pick up the wounded outlaw. Harrington also notified the engineer of an oncoming freight train to be on the lookout for the body of Black Jack Ketchum.

At daybreak on the morning of August 17, 1899, the brakeman of the slow-moving freight had been dispatched to the cupola of the caboose as a lookout. As the train approached the vicinity of the attempted robbery, he saw a bloody figure lying about 300 feet from the tracks. Then he watched in amazement as the wounded man sat up and waved a bloody hat.

The train choked to a halt.

The engineer, conductor, brakeman, and fireman walked up to the wounded outlaw. While they were standing over him, Ketchum threw down on them with his bloody revolver.

"Put up your hands," he ordered.

The engineer asked him if his idea of an honorable man was one who'd call people out to help him—and then shoot them.

Ketchum's answer was later flashed verbatim across America by the Associated Press. "No, I guess not," the outlaw was quoted as saying. "I'll die out here anyway and the buzzards will eat me." He then handed his gun to the engineer.

The trainmen carried the outlaw to the caboose and made him as cozy as possible. Then the engineer opened up the throttle and sped toward Trinidad.

Ketchum told the men that his name was George Stevens and that his attempt to rob the *Texas Fast Flyer* was his first try at robbery.

No one believed him.

Thomas Edward Ketchum was born October 31, 1863, in San Saba County, Texas. This area of West Texas, known as the Concho Valley, was famous for turning out beautiful women and law-breaking men. "Black Jack" Ketchum, as he would be called later, was the most notorious outlaw to emerge from that violent land.

Tom's father was a medical doctor who died when Ketchum was five. His mother, Temperance Wydick Ketchum, went blind several years before she died in 1871.

Young Tom had two older brothers and sisters. Berry chose to follow the straight-and-narrow and became a wealthy cattleman and horse breeder. Both of Tom's sisters married respected cattle ranchers and became pillars of their communities.

Sam was ten years older than Tom. He married early and sired a child but abandoned his family three years later. The two brothers began punching cows for ranches in West Texas and northeastern New Mexico. They got to know the territory well because of the scores of cattle drives they rode on.

The brothers might have continued their peaceable existences and even acquired ranches of their own. But Tom, always on the lookout for easy money, became the trigger man in a murder-for-hire scheme.

John M. "Jap" Powers was a prosperous rancher from neighboring Tom Green County, Texas. He was also well known for being married to the most beautiful woman in the region. On the morning of December 12, 1895, Powers was ambushed and murdered near his ranch.

The Texas Rangers were called to investigate. Before they even arrived, Thomas Ketchum had relocated to New Mexico. The Rangers soon determined that Ketchum and two of his cowpoke cronies had killed Powers. They had been hired by the ranch foreman, who thought that with the death of his boss, the attractive widow would accrue to him. He later shot himself rather than face a hangman's noose.

Ketchum got a job punching cows for the Bell Ranch just west of the Canadian River. A few months later, Sam joined his brother. He brought a substantial amount of cash which Berry had given him with the stipulation that the brothers establish a cattle ranch in Utah.

Unfortunately, Sam and Tom quickly blew the money on their favorite pastimes—drinking and gambling.

In early June, 1896, they drew their paychecks, stole a large cache of supplies and several fine horses from their former employer, and hit the outlaw trail. Before leaving, Tom confided to some co-workers that they were headed to Colorado to join up with Butch Cassidy's Hole in the Wall Gang.

Along the way, they robbed a combination store and post office in the small settlement of Liberty, New Mexico. The owner, along with three Mexican employees, gave chase. Tom and Sam set up an ambush, and when the smoke cleared, two pursuers lay dead and two had fled back to town.

The area now known as the Four Corner States (Arizona, Idaho, Utah, and Wyoming) was their next stop. There the Ketchums and their gang of former Texans went on a crime spree. Horse stealing and cattle rustling were their mainstays. But robbery and an occasional murder also ensued.

Eventually, their blossoming reputations reached the attention of America's most fabled outlaw. Butch Cassidy sent word that he would be pleased to have Black Jack and his brother visit him at Robbers' Roost, his hideout in the nearly inaccessible sleek-walled mountains of central Idaho.

Black Jack was a fine figure when he arrived at the hideout. He was six feet two, lean, and weathered. He always wore a black, well-trimmed beard and mustache.

The outlaw favored blue denim trousers and flannel shirts and always wore a white hat.

He and Cassidy hit it off immediately, but because of a conflict over tactics, neither Black Jack nor Sam ever rode with the Wild Bunch. Ketchum and Cassidy disagreed on almost every issue when it came to robbing trains. Cassidy relied on his long successful experience to argue that thirteen to sixteen robbers were needed to cover unexpected contingencies. In addition, the "army" of robbers would show such a strong force that railroad employees would recognize that resistance would be futile.

Black Jack, who'd never robbed a train in his life, argued that it would be preposterous to have to split the loot sixteen ways. And if someone gets killed, he argued, the word will get out and people on the next train will be more agreeable to handing over their cash.

In early 1897, Black Jack and Sam left Robbers' Roost to put Tom's theories to the test. Joining them were two of the most murderous members of the Wild Bunch, Will Carver and Harvey Logan. The men drifted to Wyoming where they chanced upon a disabled train near Wilcox. They promptly robbed it, getting away with more than $100,000 in recorded bills.

Carver and Logan took their share of the loot and rode off into history (each died a violent death after gunning down several men). The Ketchum brothers established a permanent hideout in Baldy, New Mexico. Being inveterate gamblers, it took only a few months for their share in the robbery to disappear.

Black Jack recruited a new gang, including Irving "Black Bob" McManus.

44

In April, 1897, the gang crossed the Green River in Utah and rode into a mining camp called Castle Gate. They robbed the payroll there, netting $25,000 in gold.

For the next two months, Black Jack and Sam flooded the region with gold coins. But by July, they were broke again. Considering their successful, albeit lucky, heist of the Wilcox train, they decided that train robbery was the way to fame and fortune.

What followed were three robberies that, when the gun smoke cleared, would find both brothers dead and establish Black Jack Ketchum as one of the dumbest bank robbers in history.

On the night of July 16, 1897, Jonas Tubbs, engineer of the *Texas Fast Flyer*, left the station at Folsom, New Mexico. The terrain was flat, and Tubbs was trying to build up speed as he headed for Des Moines, some thirty miles away, when he heard someone command his fireman to throw up his hands.

Tubbs turned and saw a man in the aisle covering the fireman with a revolver. The bandit was rocking back and forth, and at first the engineer thought he was drunk. Then he realized the man was trying to balance himself because the train was shuddering violently. Tubbs decided to stop the train and jump out the window.

In melodramatic detail, he later described what happened. "About that time," he said, "I felt a cold piece of steel pressing against my head. 'Hands up!' The old familiar dime-novel cry rang out at the same instant and you can rest assured that they went up. Our new acquaintance told us to obey commands, and by way of emphasis, jabbed us in the ribs with his six-shooter. I was ordered to run slowly to a place where a number of horses were standing and a small fire burning."

Tubbs and his fireman were marched to the express car, serving as human shields to protect their captors from the express car guard. The guard threw down his gun, and the entourage boarded the train.

Dynamite was used to blow up the safe, as well as part of the roof. The bandits collected $20,000 in gold, $10,000 in silver, and a small amount of currency. "There were ten outlaws, all having the appearance of cowboys," engineer Tubbs reported. "The leader wore a mustache and beard. It makes the cold chills run up and down my spinal column when I think about it."

After the holdup, the robbers returned to their hideout, a cave south of Folsom, where they remained until morning.

Sixteen pursuers, mostly professional lawmen, picked up the trail near the railroad tracks. They tracked the outlaws to the cave, then into the mountains. About fifteen miles from their starting point, the posse thought they were closing in on their prey. But a sudden hailstorm materialized, drenching the pursuers and washing out the tracks of the robbers.

The posse rode out the storm, then headed for a ranch about seven miles away. En route, they stumbled onto an old barn. The posse found five heavily armed men huddled inside and quickly disarmed and searched them but found no money. The captives denied being robbers and explained that they were out-of-work cowboys traveling to Colorado to seek jobs on a ranch they'd heard about. None of the posse believed the five men were the train robbers, but they took them to Clayton, New Mexico, and put them in jail. It turned out that they were cattle rustlers who were wanted in Texas, and within a few weeks, they were extradited back to the Lone Star State.

It is unclear where Ketchum and his gang went following the first Folsom-Des Moines train robbery. Notorious outlaws tended to get blamed for every unsolved robbery in the territory, and Black Jack Ketchum was no exception. It was enough to elicit a $10,000 reward for Black Jack and a $5,000 reward for Sam.

On the evening of July 17, 1899, the *Flyer* was robbed a second time. One newspaper account listed the amount of stolen loot as "substantial." Sam Ketchum later specified the figure as $45,000.

Black Jack was not in on this robbery. As the gang's leader, he thought he should get a higher percentage of the proceeds. He was voted down, however, and left in a huff.

Sam was the leader of the second robbery. As soon as they got the money, the gang lit out for the rough mountain country on pre-selected horses. A posse, headed by Sheriff Ed Farr and W. H. Reno, chief of the Special Service Department of the Colorado & Southern, started out in pursuit.

The train robbers used streams to hide their tracks and emerged only where the ground was rocky. They rode for miles on flintstone ledges and caprock, leaving no trace for the posse to follow. Twenty-five miles from Folsom, the proverbial rainstorm forced the posse to retreat home.

Deputy Sheriff George Titsworth of Trinidad County, Colorado, was browsing through some items recovered from the train robbery. He came across a letter that had been torn into small pieces. Titsworth took the shreds over to a hardware store and asked to use a desk, some glue, and a large sheet of paper. The lawman pasted the bits of torn paper to the background sheet. It turned out to be from a gang member to an ex-member.

Through good detective work, Titsworth had discovered in black and white where Sam Ketchum and his followers intended to hole up and wait out the pursuit.

A train was summoned, a gangplank was readied, and the posse of sixteen led their horses into a stock car. Then the train sped southwest toward Cimarron, New Mexico.

The seven bank robbers had chosen a fortified position in Turkey Creek Canyon to make their stand. They were heavily armed, of course, but they had added a couple of improvements to their arsenal. Thanks to the advancement of munitions manufacturing, the ensuing fight would introduce smokeless powder and steel-tipped bullets. The advantages are self-evident. Each time a round was fired with smokeless powder, a halo of gunsmoke wouldn't give away the marksman's position. And the penetrating power of a steel-tipped bullet could even rip through some trees.

An Associated Press article dispatched from Springer, New Mexico, on July 18, 1899, described the gunfight:

> The fight with the train robbers in Turkey Creek Canyon Sunday evening was one of the most desperate that has ever taken place in New Mexico, famed as it is for its encounters with desperate men. It was in the nature of a duel in the rain and semi-darkness, the pursuing posse having come upon the outlaws just about nightfall. . . .
>
> The outlaws were about to go to camp, having chosen a well-fortified place, and refused to surrender at the demand of the posse. The possemen dismounted and sought the shelter of trees, Sheriff Ed. Farr, Reno, Love and Smith going to the left of the other deputies perhaps a hundred yards. Firing was at once opened on both sides.
>
> About one hundred shots were exchanged, the outlaws having the advantage of being provided with smokeless powder, which made it difficult to locate them in the gathering gloom and the downpour of rain. They also used explosive bullets. Most of the execution on the part of the robbers was done by one of the outlaws, who appeared to be a dead shot. Every time he fired, the bullet either found its mark or came uncomfortably close to one of the attacking possemen.

The unerring sharpshooter was the ex-Hole in the Waller Will Carver. He shot Sheriff Farr through a full-grown cedar tree Farr was hiding behind, killing him. He shot and badly wounded posseman Love, who later died from his wounds. Carver also wounded three other men. Sam Ketchum was wounded early in the fight, shot through the arm, and never hit anyone.

With Sheriff Farr dead and other members severely wounded, the pursuers beat a somewhat orderly retreat back to Cimarron, eleven miles away. The next morning, a reinforced posse returned to the campsite, but the outlaws had fled.

On the battleground, deputies found bloody clothes as well as a bloody hat and slicker, a pack saddle, some provisions, a frying pan, and a large coffee pot. The ground was littered with used .30- and .40-caliber cartridge cases, and at the far end of the battlefield was a dead horse. A Winchester scabbard and a rope were on the saddle. Forty pounds of dynamite were found in a box nearby.

It seemed that the score in the "Shootout at Turkey Creek," as the media called it, would read "Outlaws, 5; Lawmen, 0." But in this case, appearances would be deceiving.

Will Carver, the hardest of those hard men who had pulled off the robbery, sustained wounds which would later kill him. Bob McGinnis, whose torn up letter led the lawmen to Turkey Creek, had four bullet wounds when the shooting was over. And Sam Ketchum almost had his arm shot off by a lawman's bullet.

On July 19, 1899, the Las Vegas, New Mexico, Associated Press bureau released a report: "Up to a late hour last night no further news was received at Springer concerning the band of robbers. The entire community has been aroused by the battle with the train robbers Sunday evening, July 18th, 1899. The pursuing posse has swelled to forty well-armed men. . . ."

The outlaws stayed together for several days after the shootout. Once their immediate danger seemed over, however, they scattered.

Sam Ketchum was the first to be captured.

He made the mistake of going to a ranch near Ute Creek. According to a rancher named McBride, Ketchum rode up to his ranch and asked for food and medical attention. The outlaw was weak from loss of blood. The rancher was out hunting some of his horses, so McBride's wife fixed Ketchum something to eat. After eating, the outlaw passed out. When McBride returned, he disarmed the visitor and sent his son to Cimarron for a doctor and the sheriff. After the doctor treated Ketchum, the outlaw was taken to town and bound over for trial.

The posse was still out searching for the remaining bandits. First on their list was Will Carver, whose uncanny marksmanship had routed an entire posse of experienced lawmen.

But death beat the posse. Carver stumbled up to a cattle ranch and asked for medical assistance. A doctor was sent for, but the outlaw died before help arrived.

A few days later, on July 24, Sam Ketchum died from blood poisoning caused by his wounded arm. His body went unclaimed, and he was buried in a graveyard for inmates behind the territorial penitentiary at Santa Fe.

At the same time his brother lay dying, Black Jack Ketchum was galloping off on a fast horse out of Arizona. He'd just killed his second man in a month, and a posse of cowboys was only a half-day behind him as he crossed the border back into New Mexico.

During his flight, Ketchum resolved to replenish his depleted funds by doing something no one had ever attempted: He planned to rob a train "single-handed."

After Black Jack's disastrous attempt to rob the *Texas Fast Flyer*, he was rushed by trainmen to the San Rafael Hospital. There doctors made arrangements to amputate the outlaw's useless right arm. But Ketchum refused to give his consent. "Let death come," he was quoted as saying.

Three days later he was singing a different tune.

Blood poisoning had set in, and Ketchum said the pain was unbearable. "Go ahead, Doc, chop her off," he reportedly told the physician.

The next day, Deputy Sheriff George Titsworth snapped Ketchum's photograph. It appeared in newspapers throughout the nation with a caption expressing the outlaw's gratitude toward the surgeon. "Thanks, Doc," the caption read. "I hope I can do the same for you some day."

Ketchum was still claiming his name was George Stevens. The photograph brought lawmen from six states to Trinidad to have a go at identifying the robber. After Sheriff Tom Stewart of Carlsbad, New Mexico, and U.S. Marshall A. F. Foraker fingered the notorious outlaw at the Trinity jailhouse, Black Jack finally admitted his true identity.

As soon as Ketchum's identity was established, Arizona authorities started extradition proceedings to have him tried for murder there. But the Territory of New Mexico also wanted him and ultimately prevailed, charging him with the murders of the two pursuers he and Sam had encountered when they first got to New Mexico. He was also tried for the train robberies.

The same day that Ketchum was identified, Ezra McGinnis was booked into the Trinity jail alongside his former boss. McGinnis had been captured on a ranch 400 miles away, in southwestern New Mexico. The two were placed in separate berths under heavy guard and transported to Santa Fe on the *Texas Express*.

It was decided that Ketchum would be tried in the fall of 1900 in Clayton, New Mexico. U.S. District Judge William J. Miles would preside. District Attorney Jerry Leahy was on the docket to try the government's case. Ketchum fired a succession of lawyers appointed to represent him and ended up defending himself.

He was as unsuccessful a lawyer as he was a train robber.

Judge Mills set the date of the hanging as October 5, 1900. But a new lawyer took up the case and managed to keep it on appeal for a year. Finally, the U.S. Supreme Court rejected the appeal, and a new execution date was set for March 22, 1901.

Territorial Governor M. A. Otero then displayed his compassionate nature by staying the execution for thirty-four days so Ketchum could get his affairs in order. Saloon wags maintained the reason was to fix it so that the city of Clayton could sell more tickets to the hanging. (Indeed, tickets were sold, and the event drew a sellout crowd.)

On April 24, 1901, the prisoner was placed under the supervision of Sheriff Salome Garcia.

Ketchum was immediately taken to jail, where he requested to inspect the scaffold from which he would hang the next day. Sheriff Garcia obliged his request and led the outlaw to the gallows. On hand were a cadre of national reporters in town to chronicle the hanging. One reporter wrote that Ketchum was in possession of "his usual nerve and was in fine humor. He facetiously remarked while inspecting the scaffold: 'It looks real sturdy, but I think they ought to hang Harrington first. Then, if it works right, they can try it on me.'" Harrington was, of course, the conductor who had shot Ketchum.

It was reported that Ketchum ate heartily and slept peacefully.

At about eight o'clock on the morning of the scheduled execution, Sheriff Garcia received a message signed by Territorial Governor Otero ordering Garcia to postpone the execution for thirty days at the request of President William McKinley. During McKinley's short tenure as president (he was assassinated by an anarchist later that year), he was notorious for staying the executions of western outlaws. So the stay didn't come as a surprise.

There was just one problem. It was bogus.

An investigation early the next morning revealed that the signature of Otero had been forged and the message concocted. But the telegram caused considerable uneasiness since most citizens assumed it had been sent by friends of Ketchum. There could be a violent effort to free the outlaw.

The foremost problem with this line of reasoning was that Clayton in 1901 might have been the most chancy town in the nation from which to try to free a prisoner. It was written that there were more guns per man in Clayton than in any other town in the United States. Even four- and five-year-olds in the area were said to be crack shots. Tack on the fact that the blood-thirsty Black Jack Ketchum had no friends and the rumor was as absurd as it was unfounded.

Nevertheless, the federal marshals and local law enforcement officials responsible for guarding the outlaw went on high alert.

Sheriff Garcia, in the meantime, was puzzling over the coming execution. He had a problem. He had never even been to an execution, much less presided over one. He took several deputies to the scaffold and had them drop a 200-pound sandbag through the trap. It seemed to work fine. After trying it several more times, Garcia was satisfied.

At noon on April 26, 1901, Black Jack Ketchum ate his last meal. He requested fried chicken, and it was served up in abundance. When he finished eating, Ketchum contemptuously declined the ministrations of a Catholic priest. He sent word to Sheriff Garcia that he was ready, then promptly laid back on his bunk and pretended to fall asleep.

An hour later, Sheriff Garcia opened the cell door and said softly, "The time is now."

A large, heavily armed entourage of lawmen escorted Black Jack through the jail yard. Civilians with loaded Winchesters seemed to be everywhere.

Guests with tickets were given seats in the stockade beside the jail. Those without tickets lined the main street and waited solemnly. Some became impatient and marched back into the saloons for another drink.

At 1:18 p.m., the outlaw climbed the thirteen steps and stood erect on the gallows beside the hangman's noose dangling from the crossbeam. He wore a broad-brimmed white hat, a brown checked coat, corduroy trousers, and high-heeled boots with large spurs. For once, he was clean-shaven.

When asked by Sheriff Garcia if he had any final words to say, Ketchum shook his head. According to one reporter, "His glance fell upon the crowd and swept over the faces with a steady, fearless, challenging look that will be remembered a long time by the men who saw it. Then the notorious outlaw growled, 'Hurry it up, boys.'"

The black hood was placed over his head and pinned to his coat. Then the noose was lowered onto the hood and tightened around his neck.

Sheriff Garcia sprang the trap.

But, instead of breaking the outlaw's neck or strangling him, the rope cut off his head. Only the hood pinned to his coat prevented Ketchum's head from rolling down Main Street.

The crowd gasped, and reporters' pencils tittered.

The botched hanging of Ketchum would galvanize a flurry of criticism from across the nation, most of it directed at Sheriff Garcia. Critics maintained that the drop of six feet was too long. A hangman from Fort Leavenworth, Kansas, explained that using the rope to practice had made it as rigid as a strand of wire.

Journalists had found a controversy, and they exploited it to the hilt. For several days, headlines across the nation blazed with outrage. How could a man's head snap off during an execution? reporters demanded. It was unheard of.

Like all good civil servants everywhere, Garcia had a ready response that completely exonerated himself. "Tom Ketchum's head being severed from his body was caused by him being a very heavy man," he wrote in a letter to the *Denver Post.* "Nothing out of the ordinary happened. No bungling whatever. Everything worked in perfect order."

After the hanging, Ketchum's remains were removed to the stockade where his head was sown back onto his body by Dr. Slack.

An hour and a half later, Black Jack Ketchum took his last ride. His coffin was a white pine box. It was transported in an express wagon to the distant cemetery by four gravediggers in boiled black suits. There were no services conducted over the remains, and there was no headstone to mark his grave.

A half-hour later, the wagon returned without the box. The gravediggers went into a saloon and proceeded to get rip-roaring drunk.

Black Jack's wealthy Texas brother, Berry, refused to claim the body, and Clayton's public officials refused to sell it to the owner of a medicine show nor the curator of a museum. They also let it be known that anyone who might be tempted to disturb the outlaw's remains would meet with serious opposition.

Sheriff Garcia kept the rope used to hang Black Jack. It had been made to order of first-class Manila hemp and was fifteen feet long. The only other known remaining souvenirs are a handful of fading admission tickets which are still being bought, sold, and traded by collectors of western memorabilia.

Black Jack Ketchum, the man whose greed caused him to try to rob a train single-handedly, faded into the lore of the Wild West.

The Execution of Anthony Chebatoris

I have neither the power nor the inclination to change the sentence. If I did have the power to do so, I think it would be unfair to suggest that the people of a neighboring state are less humane than are the people of our own state of Michigan. The federal court is enforcing a federal law in Michigan for an offense against the United States, committed in Michigan.

— Federal Judge Arthur J. Tuttle explaining why Anthony Chebatoris was to be executed in Michigan, despite a state law banning executions

The hangman was drunk. In fact, the condition of Phil Hanna, veteran executioner, threatened to put a halt to the only death sentence ever carried out in the state of Michigan.

On the night of July 8, 1938, Hanna and three companions had driven from Illinois to the Federal Detention Farm in Milan, Michigan. Along the way, they'd passed the time by drinking from quart jars of home-made hooch. Hanna's eyes were watery and unfocused. Aggressive and combative, he ordered Warden John J. Ryan to allow his friends to view the spectacle.

"Your friends aren't authorized to be here," Ryan icily told him.

Hanna soundly cursed the warden, then picked up the bag with his specially-made rope and started to leave. "If they don't watch," he said, "I don't string the bastard."

Twenty-three people had gathered to view the death of the notorious convict, including Midland County Sheriff Ira M. Smith, whose task was to spring the trap door. Other witnesses included police officials, physicians, and reporters. Ryan wondered how the hangman, with seventy-one executions to his credit, thought he could bring these three clodhoppers into the prison without permission.

Hanna was an acknowledged master of hanging. Years earlier, he claimed to have witnessed an execution in which the accused had fallen through the trap and strangled slowly, gnawing his tongue to shreds. It was gruesome, and Hanna had made it his life's work to improve the "art" of hanging. For several years, he'd worked to produce a foolproof system designed to minimize suffering. He began by testing different weights to calculate the force it took to fall from the trap to the end of the rope. After many failures, he'd come upon a formula which he contended would kill without pain. In order to perfect his craft, he'd contracted with a manufacturer to produce a special rope that had the proper amount of "give."

Hanna had once given an interview to a local newspaper. "It's not a nice thing to see a man die, or to have a part in executing him," he said. "My point is that if men are to be put to death, it should be done mercifully. I'd rather supervise a hanging and have it done correctly than attend to my farm chores and read that another hanging has been bungled by an inexperienced sheriff."

But on the morning that Anthony Chebatoris, a career criminal, avowed socialist, and convicted robber and murderer, was to hang, Hanna no longer personified an idealistic, humane executioner. He was belligerent, shouting at the warden and cursing anyone who crossed him.

Warden Ryan, aware that the scheduled execution had

set off a storm of controversy that extended as far as the White House, was determined to carry it off without a hitch. At four in the morning, he called James V. Bennet, director of the U.S. Bureau of Prisons, to whom Ryan explained the situation. Bennet crisply informed the warden that no unauthorized person would be allowed to view the execution. And if the hangman was in no condition to carry it out, Ryan himself would have to do it.

The warden was terrified. "I'm against this whole business anyway," he said.

Sweating, he walked back to confront Hanna.

The sequence of events leading to this showdown had begun a year earlier. Two ex-convicts, Anthony Chebatoris and Jack Gracy, both of whom had spent most of their adult lives in penal institutions, were planning a robbery that, if successful, would set them up for the rest of their lives.

They'd learned that every Friday the Chemical State Savings Bank in Midland, Michigan, cashed the checks of hundreds of employees of the Dow Chemical Company. In August, the two drove from their homes in Hamtramck and cased the bank. They figured that at least $100,000 in small bills should be available for the taking.

Dow Chemical was founded in 1897. Its chief products were minerals such as chlorides, bromides, and brine which were mined from beneath Midland's rich soil. By 1937, the company also produced much of the nation's ethyl cellulose and polystyrene, both of which were vital to the plastics industry. Since the 1920s, the company had used the Chemical State Savings Bank as its depository for employee payrolls.

The bank, a two-story brick structure, was located at 333 East Main Street. The upstairs offices were leased to various businesses including the dental practice of Dr. Frank Hardy.

At 11 a.m., September 29, 1937, bank President Clarence H. Macomber, age sixty-five, stood at the cashier's counter talking to his twenty-two-year-old daughter, Clair. A second cashier, Paul D. Bywater, was also on duty.

Without warning, two men suddenly rushed through the front door.

Even though it was warm outside, Gracy wore a heavy overcoat to conceal a sawed-off shotgun. Chebatoris, a small, surly-looking Polish immigrant, wore a denim jacket and hat. In his hand, he held a .38-caliber Smith & Wesson pearl-handled pistol.

Gracy ran straight to Macomber and jammed the shotgun into his ribs. Although he never announced that he was robbing the bank, it was obvious. The bank president, reacting quickly, grabbed the barrel of the gun and pushed it away.

While Clair Macomber stood open-mouthed, Bywater rushed over to help his boss. Macomber had almost gained control of the shotgun when Chebatoris moved close, aimed his revolver, and fired. Macomber, hit in the back, fell to the floor. His daughter screamed and knelt to help her fallen father.

Bywater, still rushing forward, saw the robber turn toward him. Before he could react, a gunshot blasted into his stomach, ripping through his intestines. Bywater dropped and lay writhing on the floor.

Chebatoris and Gracy realized the game was up. They fled, leaving behind $70,000 in cash.

Main Street was busy with the bustle of a mid-sized city. Motorcars were parked along the sides of the road as customers came in and out of the various stores.

The robbers had parked in front of the bank. Chebatoris jumped into the driver's seat, Gracy into the passenger's side. Chebatoris cranked the car and roared off in a cloud of smoke.

Years before, Dr. Hardy—an avid hunter—had begun hauling a .35-caliber deer rifle to work in his car. Eventually, he left the gun in his office. In his spare time, he would oil it and make sure it was loaded, never thinking he'd have to use it. Hardy had been encouraged by law enforcement officials to keep the gun handy in case of a bank robbery. In fact, he'd been deputized.

Now, hearing gunshots, he peered out the window and saw two men holding guns climb into their car. Hardy moved back into his office, grabbed his rifle, and pushed open the screen window.

The robbers' car had just turned onto Benson Street, less than a block from the bank.

Hardy aimed and fired.

The bullet grazed the car's fender, sending sparks showering through the air. A second shot slammed into the driver's side door.

As quickly as he could aim, Hardy squeezed off a third round. This shot exploded the back window and smashed into Chebatoris. Disoriented, the bandit lost control of his vehicle. On the street, panicked drivers dove for cover as the car careened across the median and crashed into a sedan which was parked alongside the road.

At impact, Gracy fell out of the passenger's seat onto the pavement. Moments later Chebatoris stumbled out of the car. The robbers quickly regrouped. They stood for a moment, scanning the city as they tried to determine where the shots were coming from. Seeing a uniformed man standing on the corner, Chebatoris fired. (He later claimed he thought the man was a police officer.) Henry J. Porter, dressed in his truck driver's uniform, went down.

The two bandits saw a car heading their way. They ran to it, forced out a woman and her baby, then clambered in. But another shot from Hardy slammed into the gas tank. The men, thinking the car would explode, jumped out.

The robbers ran over a bridge that crossed the Tittabawassee River. Suddenly, a truck driven by an employee of the Nehil Lumber Company appeared. It was overloaded and going slowly. Gracy jumped on the running board and pointed his gun at the driver.

From his window, Hardy had a clear view of the truck. He placed Gracy in his sights and fired a shot that was so remarkable it is still talked about today. At between 150 and

200 yards, he hit the gunman in the head. Gracy slumped to the ground and died immediately.

Chebatoris took off on foot up the Pere Marquette Railroad tracks. After several tries, he finally managed to break into a car, but he was too exhausted to drive off. As he sat in the vehicle breathing heavily, a group of construction workers surrounded him.

Chebatoris promptly gave up.

A few minutes later, Sheriff Smith arrested the bandit and escorted him to the Midland County Jail, where he was treated for a flesh wound to his shoulder and returned to his cell.

Dr. Hardy was recognized as a hero by the media and townspeople. A modest man, he declined many of the honors passed his way. "Don't make a hero out of me," he said. "I like to hunt and I like to play bridge. Today, I'd say I like bridge better. You know, it's a funny thing, but that parked car the bandits ran into is owned by Violet Venner. Her father was the sheriff who got me to taking my gun to work."

Within hours, the Federal Bureau of Investigation had been called in. Chebatoris had attempted to rob a bank that was a member of the Federal Reserve System. The National Bank Robbery Act, passed just three years earlier, mandated that any robbery or other crime committed during a holdup of a federally insured bank would be a federal crime punishable by federal law.

On October 11, bystander Porter died, making the crime a federal death-penalty case. While the state of Michigan had abolished the death penalty in 1845, and no one had been executed there since then, the federal government was determined to put Chebatoris to death.

The case now went to federal court and sparked a struggle that reached all the way to the White House.

On October 26, 1937, U.S. District Judge Arthur J. Tuttle, a conservative Republican, called the court to order. Tuttle had been a federal judge for twenty years, having first served as a U.S. congressman. He'd suffered a personal tragedy that some claimed turned him into a workaholic. In 1903, he'd married the beautiful Beatrice Stewart. The couple had two daughters and by all accounts were happy together. Then, on August 24, 1912, Beatrice suddenly died. Doctors determined her death was caused by complications from a severe cold. Tuttle was devastated. He never remarried and threw himself into his work.

Because someone had been murdered during the attempted robbery, Chebatoris was facing death. Miraculously, Macomber and Bywater had survived, though Bywater would suffer from side-effects of his wounds for the rest of his life.

In court, Chebatoris presented as an extremely unsympathetic character. He'd spent many years in Polish prisons before immigrating to America. An article in the Fall 1998 newsletter of the Historical Society of the United States District Court for the Eastern District of Michigan described his background:

> [He] had spent fifteen of the previous seventeen years in [American] prisons. His troubles began in 1920. As a driver for the Packard Motor Car Company, he robbed a cashier on their way to the bank. He was sent to prison and paroled in 1926. He returned to prison after a second robbery and remained there for repeated offenses that marked most of his life. At the time of his arrest in Midland, Chebatoris was wanted in Pennsylvania for bank robbery and felonious assault. He was also suspected of crimes in Kentucky.

The suspect came across as arrogant, even to his attorneys. Midland jurors saw no evidence of remorse for the misery he'd caused in their city.

During the trial, prosecutors called nearly three dozen witnesses. The defense had no answer. It was obvious that Chebatoris had committed the crimes attributed to him, and on October 28 he was found guilty.

During the penalty phase, the jury debated for many hours. They eventually decided that the convicted murderer deserved the ultimate penalty. He was the first criminal in the nation to be sentenced to death under the National Bank Robbery Act of 1934.

Judge Tuttle, in his closing remarks, wrote, "It [the death sentence] was absolutely just, as well as encouraging to the cause of justice and also a deterrent to underworld. The verdict for a man who takes the life of another man could not have been just with any other penalty than death."

The execution date was set for July 8, 1938, at the federal prison in Milan. The Bank Robbery Act specified that the death sentence would be carried out in the state in which the crime was committed.

Chebatoris, thought to be a suicide risk, was closely guarded. Somehow, though, he obtained a razor and cut his wrists and throat. He was rushed to the hospital where doctors declared that his wounds were superficial. He was treated, then escorted back to the jail.

After Chebatoris was sentenced to die, Michigan Governor Frank Murphy, an avowed opponent of the death penalty, called a press conference. "I always have been, and always will be against, capital punishment," he said. "I think the time is not far distant when it will be prohibited in every state." He castigated the federal government for its insistence that the sentence would be carried out in Michigan.

The governor of Illinois offered to carry out the penalty, but federal authorities declined.

Governor Murphy was apoplectic. He called another press conference, stating, "I deplore the fact that this execution is taking place within our state. . . . It has always seemed to me that Michigan could take pride in being the first commonwealth on this earth to abolish capital punishment. I don't think it against the interests of the people of this state to oppose its revival by having the federal government come in here, erect a scaffold, and hang a man until he is dead. . . . I think the federal government should have arranged for the execution elsewhere—if it was to take place anywhere."

Judge Tuttle responded: "An able and fearless United States attorney fairly presented this case to a qualified jury of five men and seven women, all good citizens of the state of Michigan. On October 28, 1937, that jury had the courage and wisdom to return the just verdict which directed that Chebatoris be punished by death. That just verdict having been returned, the law was mandatory in three respects: namely, that the penalty should be death, that it should be by hanging, and that it should be within the state of Michigan."

The victim's widow, Minnie Porter, weighed in on the side of the Michigan governor. "I don't feel that we have the right to say whether people should be killed," she said. "It isn't up to us. There is a greater judge."

Murphy, a close friend of Franklin Delano Roosevelt, implored the president to change the decision. "It's always the poor man who has no money or power who pays with his life," the governor said. "Another criminal, who may have committed the identical crime, but who is wealthy and powerful, escapes the chair or the noose."

But Murphy's pleas fell on deaf ears. The president, perhaps bowing to popular opinion, ignored the pleas of his friend.

On his final day of life, Anthony Chebatoris refused a special last meal. A socialist to the end, he declared, "I'll eat what the other prisoners eat."

Also an atheist, Chebatoris refused the ministrations of a Catholic priest. Even so, the priest walked beside him, chanting in Latin as the murderer mounted the gallows.

Warden Ryan had finally talked executioner Hanna into performing the task by informing him that his friends could watch from the back of the prison. Ryan knew that in the darkness they would be unable to see anything from that distance.

As Chebatoris walked up stairs to the gallows, he nodded at the executioner.

"Are you Mr. Hanna?" he asked.

The drunken executioner nodded.

Chebatoris, perhaps placing his bet on a lame horse, said, "Then I know it will be a good job."

At 5:07 a.m., a hood was fitted over the prisoner's head. Silence gripped the group of spectators—the only sound was the surreal chanting of the priest.

A minute later, the trap was sprung. Chebatoris twitched several times, then was still.

A solemn doctor waited for several minutes, then checked the prisoner's pulse. It fluttered—he was still alive. The doctor checked again. And again. After the fourth check, at 5:21 a.m., the prisoner was pronounced dead.

Hanna, evidently proud of his work, told the press that it "was a dignified execution, properly carried out." What he didn't say was that immediately after the execution, he and his three friends were forcibly removed from the penitentiary by Warden Ryan and several prison guards.

Governor Murphy called the execution a "blot on Michigan's civilized record."

Dr. Frank Hardy, the man who single-handedly was responsible for the death of one robber and the capture of the other, had been invited to attend the execution. He declined, stating that he wanted to put the shooting behind him.

Although he accepted a marksmanship medal from the Saginaw Army-Navy Club and was awarded a gold medal by the Midland City Council, Hardy's children stated that he never talked about his heroic actions.

Judge Tuttle had a long and distinguished career on the bench. He died on December 3, 1944, still declaring his support for the death sentence.

In 1940, Governor Murphy was appointed to the U.S. Supreme Court by his friend Franklin Roosevelt. He became known for his liberal interpretations of the Constitution. He died in 1949.

Immediately after Anthony Chebatoris was hanged, on July, 8, 1938, his body of was carried to the Marble Park Cemetery in Washtenaw County, near Milan. Prison guards stood at attention as his body was lowered into the ground. Later, a marker was placed on his grave. It read: "Tony Chebatoris. 1900–1938. In Loving Memory." Even though he was an atheist, a cross was engraved into the stone.

4

"The Most Enterprising All-Black Town in America"

In the words of W. W. Riley, cashier in the bank, "there was a regular war" after the first shot was fired by the white man who killed Turner.
—*The Daily Oklahoman*, Feb. 24, 1932

George Birdwell was a lean, sallow-faced, ex-Pentecostal preacher who was fond of philosophizing. "Trouble hangs onto a woman's skirt," he'd say, all the while gurgling down another shot of bootleg whiskey. Birdwell had reason to be wary of women—a jealous husband had once shot him in the leg. After being fired from his church for a multitude of sins including adultery and drunkenness, the former man of God found work in the Earlsboro, Oklahoma, oilfields where the labor was hard and the pay low.

It was there he met Charley Floyd, the man who would eventually change his life. The two worked together as oil roustabouts for a few weeks until Floyd quit to find employment as a burglar, robber, and assassin.

Charles Arthur "Pretty Boy" Floyd, as he was called by the press, wasn't the brightest bulb in the batch. But he had

a catchy name, a flair for survival, and a murderous personality that caught the attention of the media. He was ruthless,
gunning down at least eleven men during his reign of terror
in the early 1930s. Three more men who crossed him disappeared and were never found.

Born in 1904, Floyd spent his childhood on the family
farm near Sallisaw, Oklahoma. Unlike his siblings, he was a
born trouble-maker. His mother blamed his early arrests for
petty theft and burglary on "the wrong crowd" that Floyd
hung with.

From 1927 to 1930, Floyd served time in the Missouri
State Penitentiary for robbing a grocery store. Shortly after
his release, he was arrested again, this time for robbing the
Farmers & Merchants Bank in Sylvania, Ohio. In the holdup,
a bank manager had been beaten nearly to death when he
refused to open the safe. While on his way to stand trial,
Floyd escaped.

He made his way to Kansas City where he joined a gang
headed by Billy "the Killer" Miller. But the gang didn't last
long. During a Kentucky bank robbery, Miller was shot to
death by Bowling Green police. Pretty Boy Floyd managed
to elude capture and made it back to Kansas City where he
was cornered by local police and Prohibition agents. In a
desperate gunfight, the outlaw killed one of the agents,
wounded two policemen, and killed an innocent black man
who made the mistake of being in Floyd's way as he fled.

With the murder of a federal agent, the heat was on.
Floyd fled to the only place where he knew he'd be safe. The
outlaw took up residence in the Cookson Hills in Oklahoma,
where he had grown up.

So far, Pretty Boy Floyd had been relatively unsuccessful
as a criminal. He'd been arrested numerous times, had
spent three years in the penitentiary, and was now a fugitive
facing the electric chair if caught.

George Birdwell's life had also spiraled downhill since
his loss of employment as a minister. He hated working in

the oil fields and spent more time drinking than working. It wasn't long until he was fired.

With a wife and two children to support, Birdwell contacted his old friend Charley Floyd and was offered the job as the outlaw's "lieutenant."

In a weird sort of way, Birdwell had found his calling. According to C. A. Burns, head of the Oklahoma Bureau of Criminal Investigation, he quickly became the brains of the gang's operations.

The former preacher learned the nuances of bank robbery and later helped make at least one innovation which might have saved his life, had he not abandoned it. He learned how to scout banks, looking for safe escape routes and trying to gauge the amount of resistance the gang might meet during a robbery. Birdwell learned which cars were best for outrunning the police. He learned that the outlaws always wore steel body armor and would try to overwhelm local cops with their firepower—each gang member carried machine guns, pistols, and, in some cases, high-powered hunting rifles, when committing their crimes.

During the two years that Birdwell was a member of the gang, Floyd's criminal pursuits became more successful. Now they were routinely picking up $3,000 to $5,000 per bank robbery, a nice sum during the Depression. Sure, law enforcement, bankers, and armed citizens sometimes fought back, but Floyd's gang always escaped. Unfortunately, they left a bloody trail in their wake. The random murders, along with the money they stole from the banking industry, made the Floyd gang Oklahoma's most wanted criminals.

It infuriated the bankers that many of the hill farmers looked on Floyd as a hero. The life of a farmer was bleak at best. Okie soil was stingy, the work back-breaking, and the rewards thin. Most farmers were lucky to clear $300 a year. And those who borrowed from banks faced the threat of foreclosure if their crops failed.

71

It was said that Floyd passed out cash to those who helped him elude the law. In one instance, he and his gang stopped at a farmhouse near the all-black town of Boley, Oklahoma. After the housewife fed the group, Floyd handed her a twenty-dollar bill. It was said that she never told any lawman about the visit.

On the other hand, bankers were determined to stop Floyd and his gang. In *The Life and Death of Pretty Boy Floyd*, Jeffery S. King writes: "In the summer of 1932, Oklahoma authorities decided to take strong action against the epidemic of bank robberies, thirty of which were believed to have been committed by Floyd in the past eighteen months. Vigilante committees were formed in many larger towns, and the Oklahoma Bankers Association posted a reward of $100 alive and $500 dead for any robber caught or killed in the act."

It was during this time that Floyd and Birdwell came up with a novel plan. Birdwell (who had never been photographed) would scout vulnerable banks, plan a robbery down to every detail, then contract with another gang to carry it out. Floyd and Birdwell would receive a percentage of the profits and wouldn't have to risk being killed in a shootout with the law or armed citizens. Numerous such robberies kept them in spending money.

Eventually, the FBI identified George Birdwell as Pretty Boy Floyd's accomplice, and a reward was placed on his head.

During the latter part of 1932, Birdwell made the fatal decision to leave Floyd's gang and strike out on his own. He was tired of Floyd's constant womanizing ("Trouble hangs onto a woman's skirt," he would tell Floyd). He was now a full-fledged alcoholic, dependent on booze for mere survival. And he felt he deserved more publicity than the somewhat dull Floyd.

Birdwell and another member of Floyd's gang, C. C. Patterson, decided to rob the First Bank of Stonewall,

Oklahoma. Patterson was from Kiowa and was wanted for murdering a deputy in Shawnee during a previous heist. The robbery in Stonewall turned out to be a dud. Birdwell and Patterson collected less than $800. And they barely escaped, using two bank employees as hostages when armed citizens gathered outside the bank. They eventually got away but spent several days trying to elude a tenacious posse.

After Stonewall, Birdwell had second thoughts about going out on his own. On November 7, 1932, he rejoined Floyd's gang and participated in robbing the America State Bank in Henryetta, Oklahoma. They netted more than $11,000, the largest amount they would ever get.

Officials at the Oklahoma Bankers Association were enraged. Eugene P. Gunn, secretary of the association, issued a statement to the press. "Floyd has been the luckiest bandit that ever lived," he said. "Do not be surprised if you read, almost any day now, that Floyd and Birdwell have been slain."

Late one night a few weeks later, Birdwell, Patterson, and a black man named Johnny "Pete" Glass were sitting around a fire drinking moonshine. Glass began to brag about banks he'd robbed. (It was likely the whiskey talking as there is no evidence that he had actually participated in any bank jobs.)

"Let me show you how a Negro robs a bank," Glass said.

Incredibly, Birdwell agreed.

The next day, he walked into the Farmers & Merchants Bank in Boley, presumably to cash a small check. Studying the layout, he noticed there were three employees and few customers. The bank would be a pushover, he decided.

But when he approached Floyd about participating in the robbery, the outlaw turned him down. Pretty Boy felt that there wouldn't be enough money in an all-black bank to justify robbing it. In addition, he'd been warned by friends that the town would fight back. Floyd attempted to talk

73

Birdwell out of the robbery. But his lieutenant, still anxious to break out on his own, was determined to try it.

During a lifetime of committing criminal acts and fighting lawmen, Floyd's instincts had saved his life many times. Birdwell, on the other hand, desperate for a big score that would enable him to break from Floyd's organization, made a miscalculation that would cost him his life.

Boley is located in rural Okfuskee County, exactly sixty-seven miles east of Oklahoma City and sixty-eight miles southwest of Tulsa. It was founded in 1903 by T. M. Haynes while Oklahoma was still part of the Creek Indian Territory. J. B. Boley and a man named Lake Moore were early sponsors of the experiment to create an all-black community. At a formal opening of the town a year later, Booker T. Washington spoke. "Boley," he announced to an overflowing crowd, "is the most enterprising, and in many ways, the most interesting of the Negro towns in the U.S."

One example of the prosperity of Boley's citizens was the success of Hillard Taylor. A seller of cotton and its by-products, in 1911 his business took in $52,900—a fortune at that time. Many Boley residents were prosperous entrepreneurs.

In 1911, the population peaked at 11,000, but the Depression hit Boley hard, and many citizens moved away.

By 1932, there were fewer than a thousand residents of the town. Several hundred farmers lived within a few miles of Boley and came into town to buy supplies and to sell their produce. Most businesses were clustered around Main Street.

One of the most well-respected men in Boley was D. J. Turner, the president of the Farmers & Merchants Bank. He'd been mayor for ten years, and was recognized as one of the most prominent African-American citizens in the state. In the early days of the town, he'd operated a drug store. There was no bank, so farmers would leave their money with Turner, who stored it in a safe in his store. His honesty was unquestioned. In the 1920s, he helped form the

Farmers & Merchants Bank and told friends that he would do anything possible to protect the money his patrons had entrusted him with. By 1932, there were two other banks in town, but the Farmers & Merchants Bank was the most popular.

It was a cold day, less than a week before Thanksgiving in 1932, when two white men entered the bank. Patterson, wearing a long coat to conceal a sawed-off shotgun, trailed Birdwell. Neither man realized that this was the opening day of hunting season and that most of the men in town were armed with shotguns and deer rifles.

Bank President Turner rose to help Birdwell. Suddenly, Turner found himself staring down the barrel of a 1911-Model Colt .45 semiautomatic pistol.

Treasurer W. W. Riley yelled, "Hey, man! Don't hurt anybody."

Birdwell replied, "We're robbing this bank! Hand over the dough, and don't pull no alarms."

Patterson produced his shotgun and held Horace Aldridge, the one customer, at bay.

In the rear of the bank, bookkeeper H. C. McCormick ducked into the vault as soon as he saw the robbers. He was sure they hadn't seen him. McCormick grabbed a .30-30 Winchester rifle from a shelf.

Turner opened a cash box and handed the money to Birdwell.

But the last bill had been slipped between two electrodes. When it was removed, the electrodes came together and an alarm began clanging. The bank and several nearby stores echoed with the siren-like wail.

Birdwell stared open-mouthed.

Finally, he glared at Turner and said, "You pulled the alarm, didn't you?"

"You bet I pulled it," Turner said, staring down the outlaw.

Birdwell cursed Turner, then shouted, "I'll kill you for that, you son of a bitch!" He aimed the gun at Turner and blasted the president to the floor. Turner, hit in the chest, both arms, and a leg, never stood a chance.

In the vault, the explosions from Birdwell's .45 seemed far away to McCormick. He edged forward and peered out in time to see his friend and co-worker fall.

Using the door for cover, he aimed the rifle and fired. The concussion deafened him for a moment. Then he heard Birdwell yell, "I'm shot!" The outlaw dropped the bag of money, swayed for a moment, then crumpled to the floor. Blood spurted from an open wound in his neck.

"Hold me," he moaned. "Hold me. . . ."

The bandit lay next to the dying Turner, their blood pooling together on the floor.

Patterson, standing near the door, was stunned by the gunfire. Like Birdwell, he'd thought the bank would be easy pickings.

But he recovered quickly and sprang into action.

Patterson leveled his gun at Riley and Aldridge. "Grab him," he screamed, pointing to Birdwell. The men each grabbed an arm and tugged the wounded outlaw to the door. Patterson followed, waving his gun and cursing at the hostages.

Pete Glass had parked the getaway car just around the corner and on the other side of the street from the bank. As soon as he heard the gunfire, he ran toward the bank. But with every second, the street was filling with armed men.

"C'mon, man!" he yelled at Patterson.

The first shots sounded from the street.

Still holding his shotgun on Riley and Aldridge, Patterson inched his head out the door. Receiving a barrage of gunfire, he quickly plunged back into the bank.

Birdwell, lying half inside and half outside the bank door, was in the way.

Patterson stuck his gun into Riley's back. "We're goin' outside," he said. He forced the frightened clerk over his partner's body.

Ignoring Aldridge, Patterson forced Riley to run interference as the outlaw fled around the corner toward the car.

Now the entire street was lined with men firing guns. They hid behind cars, wagons, and in the doorways of storefronts. In a hardware store, a clerk handed out guns and ammunition to the few citizens who didn't have them.

As they ran, Patterson poked the shotgun into Riley's back. Then he leveled it at the crowd and fired several rounds. Ducking behind his hostage, the robber pushed Riley forward again.

About twenty-five yards from the car, a volley cut Patterson down. He slid to the ground, and lay convulsing and moaning.

Riley, shaken but still alive, dove for cover.

Glass panicked and ran back to the car. But as he cranked it, volley after volley crashed into the metal. The windshield shattered and all the windows were blasted out. Somehow Glass was able to get it running.

Smoking, trailing oil, and with two flat tires, the wounded car steamed down the street.

A gauntlet of gunners blazed away.

Glass was hit numerous times. He slumped onto the seat. The car slowly limped to the curb, and stopped.

Glass was dead.

Back on Main Street, C. C. Patterson was still alive. (Doctors would later confirm that he had more than 450 pellets in his body.)

Dozens of angry citizens gathered around the downed man.

"Let's have a turkey shoot," someone said.

But J. L. McCormick, town sheriff and brother of bank bookkeeper H. C. McCormick, stepped up and persuaded the townspeople to let the law work its course.

As soon as Patterson and his hostages left the bank, several citizens rushed in and gathered up the fallen Turner. They loaded him into a car and raced the ten miles toward

Okemah and the nearest hospital. But as they neared the city limits, Turner took his last breath.

He never said a word after he was shot.

The failed bank robbery made national news. The citizens of Boley basked in the glory of having stopped one of the deadliest gangs in history. But they also had to deal with the tragedy of losing one their most beloved neighbors.

The aftermath produced some surprises.

George Birdwell died on the floor of the bank. He was taken to the morgue in Okemah where Seminole County Sheriff Charles Dove made a positive identification. Birdwell's wife and mother came to town to claim the body. He was buried in the Maple Grove Cemetery in Seminole County, Oklahoma. About fifty people attended, including Pretty Boy Floyd's wife. Several lawmen hid nearby, hoping in vain that the famed outlaw would show as well. After a quartet sang "Rock of Ages" and "Just As I Am," a somber Reverend Robert Hedrick delivered a ringing sermon. It was entitled "As You Sow, So Shall You Reap."

Charles "Pete" Glass died in the getaway car a few blocks from the bank. His wife collected his body and told law officers the story of his boast to Birdwell about "how a Negro robs a bank."

Miraculously, C. C. Patterson survived. Crippled, he served most of the rest of his life in the Oklahoma State Penitentiary at McAllister. He was finally released, and went to work at a service station in Arizona. In one of those "stranger than fiction scenarios," he became friends with H. C. McCormick, the man who killed his partner George Birdwell.

McCormick was a given a $500 reward by the Oklahoma Banker's Association and made an honorary major in the state militia. The unassuming hero received hundreds of cards, letters, and telegrams from bankers as well as ordinary citizens who congratulated him for killing the outlaw.

As newspapers gloated over the killing of the gangsters, rumor circulated that Pretty Boy Floyd would exact revenge on the citizens of Boley during D. J. Turner's funeral. Dozens of lawmen from Tulsa, Oklahoma City, and several surrounding counties were sent to protect the town.

The headline in the February 28, 1932, edition of *The Daily Oklahoman* read:

HUNDREDS PAY HONOR TO BANKER SLAIN
IN BANDITS' RAID ON NEGRO INSTITUTION.

According to the paper, "By 1 p.m. Monday, Boley, built to house 875 persons, was a steady stream of traffic, ranging from crazily sagging wagons to large motor cars. Into the little gray home where Turner's body lay in state amid banks of floral pieces trouped hundreds of friends."

Three thousand mourners made their way to the little cemetery south of Boley to pay their last respects to the beloved Turner.

"He [Turner] gave his life to guard the money of these people who had always trusted him," the preacher stated, and hundreds agreed.

After a two-hour service, the hero of Boley was laid to rest.

W. W. Riley had a slight wound in the heel, and his jacket had been singed by one of the gunshots that felled Patterson. It was said that for many years he loved telling his story to rapt listeners.

Horace Aldridge disappeared from history as abruptly as he appeared.

A prediction made by the editor of the *Muskogee Daily Press* after the shooting of Birdwell's gang proved to be prescient. In an editorial, he wrote:

The state of Oklahoma owes a debt of sincere gratitude to the little of town of Boley which made possible the permanent removal from its sordid bank

79

robbery picture of one of the state's most active criminal menaces.

In terminating the career of George Birdwell, killing an accomplice, and wounding another, Boley has accomplished at least in part something that the law enforcement agencies have been attempting to do with no success whatever—break up the Pretty Boy Floyd bank robbing ring.

Just how effective that breakup will prove remains, of course, to be seen. Floyd, unfortunately, was not present for the Boley 'job.' . . . But Birdwell is popularly credited with being the 'brains' of Floyd's bank robbing game. Without Birdwell, it may be that Floyd's robberies won't be so well planned or so precisely executed, and that the pretty one will blunder, just as Birdwell blundered into permitting matters to take the same happy course they took at Boley.

With Birdwell gone, Floyd made two crucial mistakes. First, he hooked up with Adam Richetti, a brutal thug whose instincts were to shoot first and ask questions later.

The pair committed several robberies which left a trail of dead bodies and law enforcement officials more determined than ever to capture or, better yet, kill the thugs. The second mistake Floyd made was to move back to Kansas City. Because of his presence in the city, he and his new partner were blamed for what would become known as the "Kansas City Massacre" in which four law enforcement officers and convicted killer Frank Nash were slain. (There is much debate about whether Richetti and Floyd were participants. Some evidence points to them, but none is conclusive.) He was forced even deeper underground, protected by the mob.

Eventually, Floyd became too hot even for that sordid crew, and he, Richetti, and two female companions decided to flee to Mexico. On October 22, 1934, after being involved in a car crash, Richetti was outsmarted and captured by a local lawman near East Liverpool, Ohio.

Floyd fled into the woods near the site of the crash. Running out of options, he stopped at a farmhouse and asked the housewife for a sandwich. A few hours later, Pretty Boy Floyd was gunned down by a posse near the farmhouse where he had eaten his last meal.

Santa Claus, Bank Robber

Hey, Santa, ain't you givin' away nothin'?
— One of dozens of children who followed bank robber Marshall Ratliff down the street toward the First National Bank in Cisco, Texas

At mid-morning on Friday, December 23, 1927, four men in a stolen Buick sedan raced down a Texas highway toward disaster. They intended to rob the First National Bank in the once-booming oil town of Cisco, but their plan was flawed from the beginning.

Twenty-four-year-old Marshall Ratliff was the gang's leader. A country boy from a hard-working family, he'd just been released from the state prison in Huntsville, where he'd served two years for robbing the Bank of Valera. He liked to quip that the more banks he robbed, the better he felt about himself.

Ratliff had met Robert Hill and Henry Helms behind prison walls. Hill, age twenty-two, was a bootlegger and petty thief. He had no experience at all with a "big-time" bank robbery. Helms, ten years older, was a professional burglar who trafficked in stolen property as a sideline. He was considered incorrigible by law enforcement, having already served three tours at Huntsville.

The fourth man was Louis Davis, age twenty-nine. He was a tall, rawboned farm boy who had never been arrested. He'd joined the enterprise reluctantly, after having been persuaded by his cousin, Henry Helms.

On that winter morning, Hill drove while Ratliff sat in the back seat outlining his plan for the hundredth time. To his mind, it was simple. "There's just three rules to any successful stickup," he said. "First off, you steal a fast car. Then you drive in and rob the bank." He paused to make sure they were all listening. Finally he said, "But the main thing is, you gotta be a hundred miles away before anybody outside the town gets the word."

Ratliff allowed that the stolen Buick they were driving was plenty fast. It was brand-new, with a high-powered engine, and could probably outrun any car in Cisco, including the police chief's.

At noon, the car pulled into town. The robbers circled the bank a couple of times, their idea of casing the place. First National, as it was called locally, was located on Avenue D, which was actually the town's main street. The road was a wide, brick-paved thoroughfare. Next to the bank, a small paved alley intersected Avenues D and E. Bank employees parked their cars in the alley, and residents used it as a shortcut through town. As the robbers circled the bank, they noticed two large plate-glass windows facing the main street. By now, they had committed three lethal errors.

First, they'd forgotten to gas up the car. On the trip to Cisco from their homes in Wichita Falls, 200 miles away, the big engine had guzzled almost all the fuel the bandits had started with. The gas gauge sat on empty. However, the foursome was so busy dreaming of easy money that nobody noticed.

The second error they'd made was to assume that, at noon, everyone would be at lunch and very few customers would be in the bank. Their plan called for the robbery to go quickly and smoothly. What the robbers didn't understand was that the days preceding Christmas were among the busiest of the year for bankers—and the noon hour often found First National packed, since people could make a quick deposit or withdrawal during their lunch hour.

The robbers' final mistake was the most illogical of all: Because it was only two days until Christmas, Ratliff, who had grown up in Cisco, decided to wear a Santa Claus suit as a disguise.

For some reason that was never explained, Hill dropped Ratliff off two blocks from the bank. Immediately, the brilliant red suit and outrageous white whiskers attracted attention. Children ran to Ratliff, begging for candy or gifts. Adults brought their kids close and asked him which store he represented. Under his breath, Ratliff cursed the urchins and their nosy parents and continued walking in a straight line toward the bank.

The other robbers parked in an alley a few feet away from the bank. Ratliff, followed by several children, met up with Hill, Helms, and Davis. Together, the four brushed the children away, walked around to the front, and entered through the front door.

Instead of the two or three customers they expected, there were more than a dozen people in the lobby. Some were at the counter being served while others waited in line. In addition, it seemed that every child in town had gathered outside to wait for Santa to come out.

One girl wouldn't wait.

Six-year-old Frances Blasengame persuaded her mother to follow Santa into the bank. Mrs. Blasengame stayed just long enough to see men with guns attempting to control the crowd. Then, grabbing Frances by the hand, she fled out the side door into the alley. As she reached the street, she began screaming to all who would listen that a bank robbery was in progress.

The terrified mother ran straight to Chief of Police "Bit" Bedford's office. "They're robbing the bank," she screamed. "The bank's being robbed!"

Bedford jumped out of his chair and grabbed a double-barrel shotgun. Alex Spears, a cashier at First National, had recently headed a fund-raiser among Cisco merchants to properly arm the police department. So Bedford and his deputies had an arsenal of new shotguns and large-caliber rifles to choose from.

As the chief headed toward the bank, the citizens of Cisco were arming themselves and moving to positions outside the bank. Many of them, no doubt, were thinking about the so-called "Dead Bank Robber's Reward."

A few months earlier, in response to dozens of robberies, the Texas State Bankers Association had put a $5,000 bounty on the head of any bandit killed while attempting to rob a bank. Members of the bankers association stated publicly that they "would not pay one cent for a hundred live [robbers]." On the other hand, a citizen who killed a bank robber could become a rich man.

Inside the bank, the robbery had degenerated into a confusing comedy of errors. When Santa announced that he and his companions were robbing the bank, cashier Spears laughed. Bookkeeper Jewell Poe also thought it was a joke. But soon Hill, Helms, and Davis stuck guns into their faces, and they realized that this was no laughing matter.

Hill began rounding up customers, including two twelve-year-old girls. Holding two .45-caliber semiautomatic pistols, he moved them into the corner of the bank near the window. Anyone looking in could see the robbers' guns—any element of surprise had been lost long ago.

Ratliff ordered Poe to the back of the bank to a room-sized vault. As they were walking, two more employees

86

came out from a back room. Hill covered them and forced them into the lobby.

Inside the vault, Santa held out a gunnysack that had IDAHO POTATOES stenciled across it. Ratliff ordered Poe to fill it. The banker quickly stuffed a large amount of currency and checks into the sack. Ratliff declined several rolls of coins and led Poe out of the vault. "Let's go, boys," he shouted.

It later turned out that the robbers had taken $12,200 in cash and $150,000 in checks and bonds.

Still unaware that a crowd was gathering outside, the robbers began to move toward the front door.

Chief Bit Bedford waited outside the door, holding his shotgun filled with No. 12 buckshot. His deputy, George Carmichael, stood beside him, and an estimated one hundred citizens lined both sides of the street. All were armed. Shotguns, hunting rifles, pistols, even little derringers were among the weapons the citizens carried.

Several citizens had crept into the alley, rightly anticipating that the robbers might exit from the door leading into it.

Even before the robbers came out, an over-anxious citizen fired into the bank. The slug tore through one of the plate-glass windows, shattering it.

It was only then that the robbers looked outside and saw a gauntlet of armed men extending as far as they could see.

They were trapped, and they knew it.

Exactly five minutes had passed since Ratliff and his gang had entered the bank.

The shadow of a face appeared at one of the windows. Hill and Helms saw it at the same time, and Henry Helms snapped off a .45-caliber round just above the head of the person looking in. The glass burst, the face disappeared, and then a volley exploded from outside.

As bank customers and employees began ducking underneath tables and desks, the outlaws panicked.

For some unexplained reason, Robert Hill raised his revolver and fired four rapid bursts into the ceiling.

By now, there was steady firing from the citizens and lawmen outside. The shooters seemed to be everywhere— at the front of the bank and on both sides of the building. Slugs whined through the lobby.

Santa began to herd captives who were still upright into the bookkeeping office, where there were no windows. Davis guarded the front door. This was his first action as a lawbreaker, and witnesses later said that he seemed remarkably calm.

Helms edged toward the rear door, where he could provide covering fire when his companions decided to make a run for the car.

One of the captives shouted, "The police must be here."

Santa roared back, "Everybody in town must be here!" He was very nearly correct.

Meanwhile, Chief Bedford had sent two of his officers, George Carmichael and R. T. Redies, to watch the alley.

"I'm coming from Main Street, boys," Bedford told them. "You cover me, and I'll try to get at 'em with this shotgun."

Bedford had been in law enforcement for thirty years. As sheriff of Bedford County, he'd faced down and dispersed lynch mobs with nothing but his reputation and a shotgun. He was known throughout Texas as one of the last of the old frontier lawmen—honest, courageous, and modest. "I just go where the law sends me," he once said to a reporter who had inquired about what it takes to be a lawman.

Armed men were still streaming toward the bank. Within minutes of the announcement that the bank was being held up, clerks in local hardware stores had begun passing out rifles and ammunition to any citizen who wanted them. Businessmen pulled revolvers out of desk drawers and hustled toward the crime scene. Postmaster J. W. Triplett grabbed two big semiautomatic handguns from his desk drawer, gave one to his assistant, and then the pair headed for the alley to join up with lawyers, roustabouts, clerks, and farmers.

Inside, shell casings were bouncing and spinning across

the floor as the robbers poured gunfire through the shattered windows.

Then Santa had a brainstorm born of desperation.

With well-placed firepower, the robbers were doing a pretty good job of keeping the alley clear, but Ratliff knew they'd soon be out of ammunition. It was time to move.

He groped around under a big table and began to yank out citizens who had been hiding there. "The only chance we got is right here," he said. What he meant was that the bandits were going to use the employees and customers as human shields.

The first to be pulled out from under the table was bookkeeper Vance Littleton. His assistant, young Freda Stroebel, was next. Even though he was holding guns in both hands, Santa grabbed Freda and pushed her to the back door. Ratliff's accomplices began rounding up the other hostages.

Alex Spears, the head cashier, decided to make a dash out the back door. A shooter, waiting in the alley for the robbers to come out, quickly put a bullet through the banker's jaw. Spears fell back into the bank as blood gushed from his face. "I can't go," he moaned. "I'm bad hurt."

Robert Hill cursed the banker. Then he said, "You'll go, or you'll die right here." The outlaw jammed the barrel of a revolver into Spears's ribs and again forced him to the door.

The robbers, using their pistols as clubs, eventually herded sixteen people out the back door into the alley. Then they began to push or pull them toward the waiting Buick. The one thing the outlaws had going for them was that the townspeople didn't know which car they were headed for.

Helms came out first, surrounded by hostages. Davis, the farm boy, came out next. He was halfway to the car when a blast from a shotgun caught him dead-center in the head. He was knocked backward but managed to pull himself upright. Then he staggered and fell into the car.

Robert Hill was the third robber to exit the bank, and he pushed bookkeeper Littleton in front of him. The townspeople stopped shooting for a moment, and Littleton broke free and ran toward safety. Hill hopped around the Buick and jumped into the driver's seat.

Spears, bloody and terrified, raised his hands above his head. "Get in the car", someone commanded him. But the banker veered off down the alley and ran around a corner of the bank. He ducked into a narrow passageway and became the first hostage to reach safety.

Hostage Marion Olson, a Harvard law student who was home for the summer, was hit in the shoulder almost as soon as he stepped outside. He tried to run back into the bank but was stopped by a gunman and pushed into the back set of the car. Hunched in the back seat, Olson calmly announced to his captors, "I'm shot. I've got to go to the hospital." Then he simply opened the back door and walked up the alley toward the medical care that he urgently needed. He would spend the next two weeks in an intensive care unit.

Santa was the last holdup man to come out of the bank. Freda Stroebel was in front of him, and he was firing over her shoulder. At the car, he pitched the potato sack into the back seat and ordered the young bookkeeper to get in. Instead, she scampered away and took the same avenue of retreat that Spears had taken. She was uninjured, an incredible piece of luck considering the number of rounds that had whizzed by her.

Oscar Cliett, a grocer, took a bullet through the heel on his way out of the bank. The 300-pound man stumbled to a light pole and somehow survived the crossfire without being hit again.

The first-cage teller, Jewell Poe, came out the door and ran for his life.

Two girls, Laverne Comer, age twelve, and Emma May Robinson, ten, had been inside when the bank was held up. Laverne and her sister had raised some cows together and had deposited the earnings from the animals' sale in a joint account at First National. With Christmas just two days away, Laverne had gone to the bank to withdraw her share of the proceeds so she could get her sister a present. It had befallen teller Poe to hesitantly explain to the little girl that she would have to get her sister's signature before she could withdraw any funds from the account. Laverne and her chum Emma May were trying to think of a solution to that dilemma when the robbers took over the bank.

Now the terrified girls, who had been pushed into the alley with the other hostages, wailed as bullets flew all around them. Henry Helms grabbed the pair and growled, "Get on the fender." He thought that the townspeople might be less inclined to shoot at the Buick if a couple of their children were conspicuously exposed.

But when the girls refused to move, Helms roughly shoved them into the back seat still wet from Marion Olson's blood. Santa Claus was still standing by the door. All the hostages had escaped, so Santa was momentarily alone. Chief Bit Bedford and officer George Carmichael advanced toward him from the east and of the alley. Bedford aimed his spanking-new 12-gauge pump and pulled the trigger—but nothing happened.

The expensive shotgun had jammed. As Bedford frantically worked the pump mechanism to dislodge the shell, Santa snapped off two rounds at him. The shots missed the six-foot-four, 220-pound target. Bedford finally cleared the weapon and boomed a blast at Santa, but at the moment he fired, a round tore into his abdomen. Bedford dropped the shotgun and fell backward onto the brick lane. He was reaching for the Colt revolver strapped to his leg when he lost consciousness.

From the west end of the alley, deputy Carmichael charged toward the Buick. A volley from the car found its mark, and Carmichael went down about ten yards from where his chief lay dying.

Miraculously, all four bank robbers had made it inside their getaway car. Hill and Helms were in the front seat, with Laverne Comer wedged in between them. Louis Davis was gulping his last breaths in the rear, his bloody head slumped on the plush gray upholstery. Marshall Ratliff sat beside him, holding Emma May Robinson on his lap and clutching the sack full of paper in his hand.

The mob of townspeople formed two lines through which the robbers would have to pass. After Bedford and Carmichael went down, their collective mood seemed to change. At first, defending their bank and their town had seemed like an honorable adventure. Now the citizens of Cisco were angry.

In the Buick, Robert Hill frantically pumped the gas pedal and subsequently flooded the engine.

Alex Spears, still bleeding from the hole in his jaw, had returned to join in the shootout. He rushed over and snatched up Carmichaels's revolver, aimed at a figure in the Buick, and was about to pull the trigger when he saw the two little girls. He lowered his firearm and ran back down the line warning the townspeople that the robbers had female captives.

R. L. Day, a café cook, had borrowed a semiautomatic shotgun from a clerk in a hardware store. He ran up to the car, aimed at the driver's face, and pulled the trigger. Nothing happened—Day didn't know how to click off the safety. The robbers' luck was still holding. Day was still squeezing the trigger when Hill finally got the car going.

The Buick lurched off down the alley, picking up speed as it headed west. Postmaster Triplett had been biding his time. As the getaway car passed, he fired six rounds at it. One of the bullets flattened a rear tire. The automobile swerved from the alley onto Avenue D so violently that a rear door flew open. Santa and Emma May were almost thrown out of the vehicle.

The sedan turned south. At least a dozen men chased it on foot. Ratliff broke the rear window and fired through it.

From the front seat, Helms threw roofing nails out the window. This pathetic attempt to slow the pursuit had been born in Huntsville as prisoners talked among themselves about the best way to stage a bank robbery. Like most of their other efforts, the nails did little to slow the determined citizens.

Davis was in a state of shock. His head lolled on the back of the seat, and his eyes rolled wildly from side to side.

With its flat tire, the Buick wandered all over both lanes of Avenue D. Oncoming cars jumped the curb as their drivers bailed out rather than risk a head-on collision.

Then, as the Buick clip-clopped down Avenue D, there came a brief moment that may have been the most poignant in this whole sorry episode. Three blocks south, a blind fiddler sat on a small canvas stool scratching Christmas carols out of his instrument. Beside his foot was a gray felt hat for listeners to drop coins into. When the gunfire started, his audience quickly melted away. Now, as the Buick came up the avenue toward him, he broke into a hysterical rendition of "Soldier's Joy." The closer the Buick came, the faster he scraped. Not knowing where to go, he continued playing as bullets buzzed about him.

The Buick soon left the foot pursuers in the dust. But dozens of other people quickly jumped into their cars to continue the chase.

Inside the bandits' car, things were grim. Davis was wavering between life and death, and Ratliff was bleeding badly from a wound in his jaw. He wasn't sure when he'd been hit—it may have been as he was getting into the car.

Then Hill, trying to steer a big car with a flat tire, looked down and noticed the fuel gauge sitting squarely on empty.

"We gotta get another car," he screamed.

"Not till we get to another town," Ratliff replied.

Hill paused and looked at the gauge once more to make sure he was right.

"We're outta gas," he said.

Silence.

It was at this point that the bandits knew they were doomed.

But they wouldn't give up without a fight.

On Fourteenth Street, near the outskirts of Cisco, Ellis Harris and his family were cruising in their nifty new Oldsmobile. Fourteen-year-old Woody was driving. His grandmother sat beside him and his parents sat in the back. At Avenue D, the boy saw Santa Claus waving for him to stop.

He hesitated. Then his mother, thinking it must be some kind of Christmas stunt, told Woody to see what Santa wanted. He pulled to a stop, and his mother quickly realized her mistake.

"Get out of that car!" Hill ordered, waving his gun in Woody's face.

Nobody budged.

"Get them out, Henry," Santa yelled. "The road's filling up behind us."

Helms reached through the window and placed his pistol against the head of Woody's grandmother, but she turned her head away and remained seated. Robert Hill finally ran around the car and picked her up and stood her on the sidewalk.

Santa hustled up to the driver's window and informed young Woody that he'd take over the driving. The boy politely nodded. Then he took the keys from the ignition, put them in his pocket, and jogged over to a nearby house. The first question he asked his mother, who was now hiding behind the same house, was why Santa would hang around with hoodlums.

The robbers began to move everything they had from the Buick to the Oldsmobile. They forced the two girls, Laverne and Emma May, out onto the sidewalk. The friends stood there, too terrified to run.

The men toted Davis from the shot-up Buick and placed him in the back seat of the Olds. Then they tossed the sack containing the money in beside him. Finally, the girls were herded into the front seat.

The motorcade of angry citizens was only a block behind but suddenly stopped. From a block away, men with rifles began taking potshots at the robbers. At some point during this fusillade, Bob Hill was shot in the shoulder.

His wound was painful but far from lethal. Hill jumped into the driver's seat. It was then that he realized he had no keys. When he told the others, Ratliff said they should hotwire the car. The posse's firepower, however, prevented the outlaws from opening the hood.

"Oh, Jesus!" Ratliff swore.

After a couple of minutes of indecision, a migration began back to the crippled Buick.

To thwart the posse, the two girls were steered out in front by the robbers. As Ratliff, Hill, and Helms rushed back to the getaway car, Hill asked about their comrade who was dying in the back of the Pontiac.

"Let him stay," Ratliff said. "He'll have a better chance with them than with us."

Helms disagreed, but things were moving too fast.

Hill managed to get the nearly gasless Buick with the flat tire moving again. Then someone mentioned the money. The air seemed to go out of the robbers. They'd forgotten the sack—it was in the Oldsmobile.

As soon as the Buick pulled away, the townspeople descended on the Olds. The crowd proclaimed Woody a hero for thwarting the robbers. They took Davis back to town, where law officers interviewed him in his hospital bed. The mortally wounded farm boy told his interrogator his name but steadfastly refused to identify his companions. He died later that night, a sad testament to the influence of his uncle, Henry Helms.

A few rooms down, Chief Bit Bedford was also dying. As he swung between comas and incoherence, Cisco's long-time motorcycle patrolman, Harvey Olman, became acting police chief by default.

After capturing Davis and recovering the bank money, Cisco began to count its casualties. Bedford and Carmichael were dead or dying; Alex Spears's jaw was partly shot off; Marion Olson was in the intensive-care unit; Oscar Cliett had been shot in the heel; and Pete Rutherford had suffered a clean wound through his thigh. R. L. Day, the inept shot-gunner, had been nicked along his scalp by a ricochet.

A reporter for the *Fort Worth Star Telegram* had witnessed the gun battle. He stated that it had lasted fifteen minutes, a time span that many of the participants thought was too brief.

Back in the Buick, Helms turned off onto a dirt road near the city limits sign. He followed it for about three miles until it played out, after which he gunned the car into some dense brush. As the robbers prepared to flee on foot, Santa took off his mask to assess his bloody jaw.

Laverne and Emma May were ordered not to look, but Laverne dared to sneak a peek. Even though she was rewarded by a sharp smack on the skull by Helms's .45, she'd seen enough to recognize Santa as a local ne'er-do-well named Marshall Ratliff.

The girls were ordered to lie on the bloody floor of the Buick. They held each other, shivering and sobbing as the bandits fled. As usual, the fugitives had forgotten to take their provisions (four loaves of bread, a canteen of water, and a can of coffee).

The posse quickly came upon the Buick. Once the girls were rescued and Ratliff had been identified, one of the largest manhunts in Texas history began.

The Texas Rangers were brought in, and to assist them, bloodhounds and cropdusting airplanes were deployed. In addition to the lawmen, more than a thousand citizens were out beating the bushes.

For the hunters and the hunted, things went bad quickly. The temperature dropped into the twenties, and icy winds blasted through the brush.

The major concern of the robbers was not that they might be spotted—it was how far could they walk, wounded and bleeding, without food or water, and with the bone-crushing cold whipping through their light jackets, squeezing their spirits with every gust.

They stayed out for three days before they finally took a chance and walked up to an isolated farmhouse about thirty miles from Cisco. There they kidnapped teenager Carl Wylie so that they could use his car. After twenty-four hours, the outlaws stole another car and released Wylie. The teenager reported to authorities that all of the bandits were severely wounded, malnourished, and dispirited.

After several days during which lawmen were sometimes only minutes behind the fugitives, Texas Ranger Cy Bradford and a select posse of lawmen and citizens ambushed the three robbers in Young County near the Brazos River. In the firefight that followed, Ratliff was again wounded. Unconscious and near death, he was rushed to a local hospital. Helms and Hill ran into a nearby forest and managed to hide for two more days. They were finally captured in the small town of Graham.

Ratliff eventually recovered from his wounds, as did Helms and Hill.

At the trials that followed, the prosecutors asked for the death penalty for Ratliff and Helms.

Helms was identified as the gunman who had shot both Bit Bedford and George Carmichael. He was sentenced to death. After unsuccessfully feigning insanity while awaiting execution, he was electrocuted at Huntsville prison.

Ratliff was also sentenced to death, but he met his end in a slightly different way. After being extradited to Eastland County for a hearing to determine if he was truly insane, Ratliff attempted to escape. In the process, he murdered a much-loved jailer named Tom Jones.

The citizens of Eastland County had had enough. An enraged crowd gathered outside the jail and overpowered Sheriff Pack Kilburn, who was attempting to hold back the mob. The crowd pulled Ratliff from the jail and hanged him from the nearest telephone pole.

Robert Hill pleaded guilty and was sentenced to ninety-nine years in prison. After serving twenty-five years, he was paroled. Hill changed his criminal ways and became a law-abiding citizen.

Although a grand jury investigated the lynching of Marshall Ratliff, no one was ever tried for the crime.

The $5,000 reward was never collected.

Kraft State
Bank Robbery

James Kraft, 21, assistant cashier and son of Mr. and Mrs. W. P. Kraft, was taken with the bandits as a shield for bullets after they had robbed the Kraft State Bank here Tuesday. The young banker was later found slain in a ditch on a side road on Highway 23 with a bullet hole in the back of his head.
— *The Dunn County News*, Oct. 22, 1931

On December 25, 1930, the Kraft State Bank in Menomonie, Wisconsin, ran the following large advertisement in *The Dunn County News*:

BULLET-PROOF CAGE GUARDS BANK.
We are not inviting holdups through inadequate protection, this bank is installing a bullet-proof armored cage, overlooking every part of the lobby, tellers cages and the only exit, leading out to Main Street.

This bullet-proof cage is absolutely impregnable against machine-gun or rifle fire, and will be manned by expert riflemen, summoned in time of need by automatic alarms conveniently located. These alarms will not only call guards to man the cage, but also notify employees in the Berg Chevrolet Company, Montgomery Ward & Company, and the Farmer's Store, where marksmen are instructed to obtain a full view of the entrance to the bank.

The installation of this modern method of bank protection, in reality "fighting fire with fire," is just another step of the Kraft State Bank to safeguard its depositors' money. An expert marksman in the armored cage is prepared to meet every possible hold-up emergency, giving us an absolute security against bandits.

Although every dollar of our depositors' money is fully protected against insurance, that is no reason for inviting a hold-up through inadequate protection."

If the ad was supposed to deter robbers from attacking the bank, it failed miserably. In fact, had certain bandits been familiar with the small-town newspaper, the holdup they attempted on October 20, 1931, might have been less bloody.

The Kraft State Bank was established in 1914 by Phillip Kraft and his sons, John, William, and Samuel Kraft. The bank sat on the south side of Main Street, in Menomonie, between Montgomery Ward and the Meat Market. The southern shore of Lake Menomin lay directly across Main Street.

The bank was a two-story, red-brick structure. The front door led into the lobby—behind the counters was a room-sized safe and several offices.

On Tuesday, October 20, at 9 a.m., life in Menomonie was humming along as usual. The talk among young people was about the "human fly" who had scaled the Marion Hotel the night before. Babe White, a daredevil from Chicago, had put on a show as children gawked and teenagers feigned indifference.

To the many farmers who lived around the town, the conversation inevitably turned to Man O' War, a local Holstein bull that had recently won the All-American Championship at the National Dairy Show in St. Louis.

The Associated Charities of Menomonie had scheduled a drive for the needy on Saturday, and on the same day, the County Settlers Reunion Committee planned its annual dinner replete with old-time fiddlers and story-tellers.

At about 9:15 a.m., a 1928 Lincoln Sport Phaeton pulled up to the curb in front of Frank Hintzman Funeral Parlor, which was less than a block from the bank. The car was top of the line. Swift but elegant, it could hold seven passengers and reach speeds of seventy-five miles per hour. It was much faster than the cars most police departments owned.

Inside the bank, ten customers and five bank employees were conducting business.

Bank guard Vernon Townsend watched three men walk through the front door. He immediately saw that they were not "normal" customers. All wore heavy coats with bulges which might conceal firearms. Townsend tripped an alarm, then raced upstairs. The alarm began ringing in nearby stores, including the Farmer's Store and the Lakeside Café.

Townsend found a nook on the roof and settled in with his sidearm to wait for the bandits to come out. Later, when asked why he hadn't fired at them while they were inside, he said that his orders were not to shoot inside the bank.

Those in nearby stores heard the alarm and quickly armed themselves. Winfield Kern, owner of the Lakeside Café, grabbed a pistol and moved to the front door of his restaurant. Ed Grutt and Paul Gregg were in the Gregg Music Store, which was located in the second story above the Farmer's Store. Grutt grabbed a rifle, moved back to the window, and waited for the robbers to come out of the bank.

Ed Kinkle, also in a nearby store, grabbed a rifle and positioned himself so that he could see the entrance to the bank.

As soon as the alarm sounded, the lookout drove the Lincoln directly to the front of the bank. Wearing a charcoal-gray coat, he was described by witnesses as standing five

101

feet ten and weighing nearly 175 pounds. The driver parked, grabbed a machine gun, got out, and fired a few rounds.

By now, the town was in an uproar. It seemed that everyone knew a robbery was taking place.

In Municipal Court, Frank Sweeney was being tried for driving while under the influence. Chief of Police Louis Frenstad, attending the trial, was called away, and the court hearing was postponed.

Back on the street, the lookout stood in front of the car holding his machine gun. Waving it back and forth, he made it clear that he was ready to shoot anyone who moved.

As soon as the three robbers rushed into the bank, they pulled machine guns from their coats and screamed for everyone to get down on the floor.

One robber, later identified as Preston "Charlie" Harmon, rushed up to cashier R. A. Rommelmeyer. As Harmon scooped cash from the teller's drawer into a bag, the others trained their guns on the hapless victims.

Like all the employees and customers, William R. Kraft, the twenty-four-year-old son of Mr. and Mrs. W. F. Kraft, lay on the floor. He'd been a few feet from the door of the vault when the robbers blew in, and he dropped down where he stood. Harmon stepped over Kraft and rushed into the vault. He grabbed stacks of bonds and stuffed them into the bag. A later accounting of the bank's losses showed that the robbers got $2,973.42 in cash, $87,000 in registered bonds, and $7,940 in negotiable bonds. (The registered bonds could not be cashed unless they were approved by the bank's board of directors; thus, they were useless to the robbers.) When Harmon stepped out of the vault, he told Kraft, "There's more money here. I want it."

Kraft looked up and replied, "You've got it all."

The robber pulled a .45 semiautomatic pistol from his coat. At point-blank range, he fired. The bullet pierced Kraft's left shoulder and came out his chest, barely missing his heart. Even so, the bullet punctured a lung.

As soon as the shot was fired, all three robbers bolted for the door. Along the way, they grabbed two hostages, James Kraft and Mrs. A. W. Schafer, a clerk.

As they raced from the bank into the street, townspeople began firing. The lookout returned fire. Bullets sprayed the window near Winfield Kern, still at the front door of his café. As the bandits pushed Mrs. Schafer along, she stumbled and fell onto the sidewalk. In their panic, they didn't pick her up.

Kern, Grutt, Kinkle, bank guard Townsend, and several other townspeople leveled a withering fire at the outlaws. They took care not to hit young Kraft. Someone heard the lookout scream in pain as he ducked into the car. Taking Kraft with them, the bandits piled inside, and the heavy Lincoln screeched away. More townspeople were firing now—in fact, a barrage of projectiles raked the car as it fled.

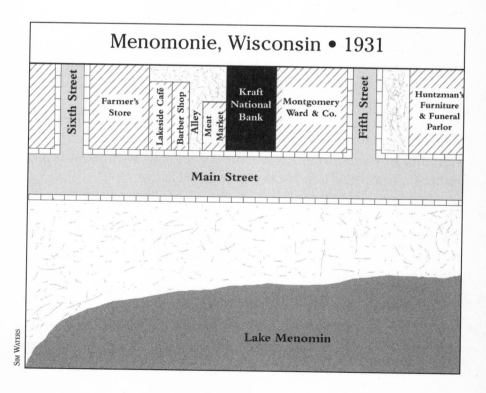

103

The Lincoln headed east on U.S. 12, then turned north on County Trunk B. Behind them, Sheriff Ike Harmon and a group of armed citizens leaped into their own cars and roared off in pursuit. The cars of the townspeople were no match for the high-powered Lincoln, however. To further slow the pursuers, the outlaws began pouring nails and tacks onto the road.

As the Lincoln outdistanced the pursuers, two of the bandits were in deep trouble. The lookout, a gangster named Frank Webber, screamed in pain from a bullet that had penetrated his eye. A few minutes after the robbery, he died.

Now the robbers turned onto the Old Suckow Road, heading east. Near the Ranney farmhouse, they stopped and tossed the body of Webber from the car. Perhaps in retribution, they forced James Kraft, their captive, from the car and shot him in the back of the head.

After scattering more tacks onto the road, the gangsters headed north toward Wheeler. They'd planned their escape route meticulously, hiding five-gallon gas cans every few miles along the route. Through Boyceville, Prairie Farm, and Clear Lake, they pressed on.

Their pursuers were disorganized and never got close. In less than an hour, however, the posse came upon the grisly remains of Kraft, blood from the fatal head wound darkening the ditch in which he lay.

Webber, his corpse lying on the road, had two pistols in his pants and wore body armor. A second steel vest was found on the road near the corpse. An examination of his wounds showed that Webber had been shot in the temple, and the bullet had exited through his right eye socket.

(Two years later, a .32-caliber Harrington & Richardson revolver was found by a farmer in the field near the location where the bodies had been dumped. Two notches had been cut into its grip. It is thought by local historians to have been one of the guns used by the bank robbers.)

PHOTO COURTESY OF FRANK KENNETT
AND DUNN COUNTY HISTORICAL SOCIETY

This .32-caliber H & R revolver, found two years after the Menomonie bank robbery, may have been used to murder James Kraft. Discovered in a field near where Kraft's body was dumped, it has two notches cut into the grip.

Several pursuers carried the news of Kraft's death back to town, where hundreds of enraged citizens armed themselves and took to their cars in hopes of locating the robbers so they could dole out some vigilante justice.

Coroner Carl Olson arrived at about noon. He pronounced Webber and Kraft dead, and authorized the removal of their bodies to the funeral home.

The robbers continued north.

Near Shell Lake, they dumped a second body from the car. When the pursuers arrived on the scene, they found a stack of securities near the corpse, as well as two revolvers and a machine gun. The dead man was later identified as Charlie Harmon, the robber who had stuffed the money in the bag. He'd been hit in the neck and the knee.

When he was examined by the coroner, buckshot found in his body showed that he had been in other gun battles.

After Harmon's body was found, the robbers' trail dried up. The men of Menomonie had taken out two of the four bank robbers, but because of the death of James Kraft, they wanted to identify the other pair and bring them to justice.

Charlie Harmon liked to play golf and had joined several exclusive courses. The Texan was fond of bragging about his expertise in the sport, but he seldom seemed to win. He pouted and whined when he lost, which was often. Harmon had started his criminal career in Texas when he robbed a gambling hall. He was sentenced to prison, then migrated north upon his release. He ended up in Chicago, a corrupt town where politicians were known for protecting criminals and where most policemen were on some gangster's payroll.

It was there that the Texan fell in with Frank "Jelly" Nash, "Tough" Tommy Holden, and Francis L. "Jimmy" Keating. On September 10, 1926, the quartet robbed a Grand Trunk Railroad train of $135,000. The gang was dubbed the Evergreen Bandits by the media because they stopped the train in Evergreen Park, Illinois.

Members of the gang were identified, tracked down, convicted, and sentenced to the federal penitentiary at Leavenworth, Kansas. Nash, Harmon, and George "Machine Gun" Kelly helped Keating and Holden escape. Harmon also escaped in a later jailbreak. He rejoined his gang in another corrupt town, St. Paul, Minnesota. Along with their new partner, Webber, the gang drove a circuitous route to Menomonie, leaving five-gallon cans of gasoline at abandoned farms along the way.

Although they had planned the robbery in detail, they didn't count on the tenacity of the citizens of Menomonie.

The trip proved a one-way ride for Charlie Harmon and Frank Webber.

The criminal lives of Keating and Holden were so interconnected that their band was called the Keating-Holden Gang.

For nearly two years they terrorized the Midwest, committing a string of stunning robberies and murdering anyone who got in their way. This gang had many members who floated in and out as needed, including the infamous Harvey Bailey, Alvin "Creepy" Karpis, Verne Miller (architect of the Kansas City Massacre), Bernard Phillips, and Big Phil Courtney.

On July 15, 1930, the Keating-Holden Gang robbed a Willman, Minnesota, bank of $70,000.

On September 9, 1930, the bandits took $40,000 from a bank in Ottumwa, Iowa.

Then, on September 17, 1930, they literally struck gold, committing the most successful bank robbery of the gangster era. They hit the Lincoln National Bank & Trust Company in Lincoln, Nebraska, for a whopping $2.5 million.

On October 2, 1931, the gang robbed the First National Bank in Duluth, Minnesota of $58,000.

After being decimated in Menomonie, the gang recruited new members and looted the Northwestern National Bank in Minneapolis of $266,000 in cash, coins, and bonds.

In between the robberies, the gang was suspected of having committed several murders, including those of two molls, Indian Rose Walker and Marjorie Schwarz. The gang suspected the women of informing the police of their whereabouts. The molls—both with gunshot wounds to the head— were found in a burning car that was later traced to Karpis.

On June 17, the Citizens National Bank in Fort Scott, Kansas was robbed of $47,000.

Two weeks later, the FBI received a tip that the gang members would be playing golf at the Old Mission Golf Course in Kansas City. Agents descended on the course, arresting Keating, Holden, and Harvey Bailey, who still had one of the notes from the Fort Scott robbery in his pocket.

Keating and Holden were sent back to Leavenworth to serve the remainder of their twenty-five year sentences. Bailey was tried and convicted of the Fort Scott robbery and sent to the Kansas State Prison, from which he promptly escaped.

Tommy Holden was an incorrigible inmate and was transferred from Leavenworth to the federal penitentiary at Alcatraz. He was paroled in 1948 and moved back to Chicago. In 1950, he murdered his wife and two of her brothers. He went on the run but was tracked down in 1951 after being put on the FBI's newly established "Ten Most Wanted" list. He spent the rest of his life behind bars at the Illinois State Penitentiary in Joliet, where he died of a heart attack in 1953.

Jimmy Keating turned his life around after being transferred to Alcatraz. He worked hard and was released in 1948. Keating moved to Minneapolis, where he worked as a florist. He remarried and became a union representative. Keating died in 1978.

Neither man was ever tried for the unprovoked murder of James Kraft.

After a long hospitalization, William R. Kraft, the assistant cashier who was shot in the shoulder, recovered from his wound.

One of the legends that sprang up after the Menomonie gun battle is that restaurateur Winfield Kern had become so excited that he shot through the windows of his own café. However, two weapons experts later examined the glass and concluded that the bullet holes were entry holes, meaning the shots had come from a bandit's weapon.

Although it's almost impossible to tell who shot the robbers, evidence suggests that Ed Grutt, firing from the upper windows of the music store fatally wounded Charlie Harmon. Either Winfield Kern or Ed Kinkle probably hit Webber. This is based on the fact that Harmon, the lookout, was heard to yell "Ouch" as he jumped into the car, and at that point, Kinkle and Kern were both firing at him.

What about the bullet-proof cage that supposedly guarded the tellers? The Kraft State Bank advertisement in *The Dunn County News* had specifically stated that the bullet-proof cage was "impregnable against machine-gun or rifle fire." If that was true, the gangsters were able to move around the cage and get into the teller's area.

According to the ad, the cage would hold "expert riflemen," who would be sufficient to hold off any robbery attempt. In fact, Vernon Townsend was the only guard on duty, and he was under orders not to fire inside the bank. While he did pull the alarm and engaged the robbers in the gunfight outside the bank, he was not the expert marksman the ad claimed was available.

On the other hand, the bank had indeed made arrangements with nearby businesses to lend firepower in case of a robbery and had also installed an alarm system to alert others to any robbery in progress.

It is likely that, given the large number of bank robberies that were occurring in Wisconsin (there were thirty-four such heists in the state during 1931 alone), the officers of the Kraft State Bank sought to allay their customers' fears by placing the ad—and if they exaggerated somewhat, so be it.

In the final accounting of the Menomonie bank robbery, two murderous desperadoes were killed by armed citizens.

Unfortunately, James Kraft also died, and never received the justice he deserved.

Henry Starr's Last Ride

You work with me, and I'll work with you.
— Henry Starr's instructions to bank employees
before being shot by banker William J. Myers

On the morning of February 18, 1921, a Nash town car stopped near the Crooked Creek Bridge on Main Street in Harrison, Arkansas. A cold rain the night before had puddled the dirt streets. Now sleet formed icicles around the edges of the puddles.

The bridge was about 200 feet from the center of town, and less than that from the People's National Bank. The bank was a massive two-story brick structure. Offices on the second story housed a physician, architect, and other businesses. The first floor housed the bank.

At 10 o'clock three men walked into the bank. As they entered the door, they tracked mud and ice across the floor. Wearing heavy coats, two of the men walked to the counter while the third waited at the bay window overlooking the street.

When cashier Cleve Coffman looked up, he saw that one

of the men was pointing a rifle at him. The gunman's hat was tipped over his forehead, and he wore spectacles. The attempted disguise struck Coffman as ridiculous.

"Keep quiet and don't move," the man hissed.

At the same time, a second man began forcing customers from the lobby into the cubicle behind the counter.

Bank President Marvin Wagley, also manning a customer window, stared at the robbers in disbelief.

The man holding the rifle walked around the wall that separated the cubicle from the lobby. He moved over to Wagley. "Where's the cashier?" he demanded.

Wagley hesitated, and the man punched him in the ribs with the barrel of his rifle.

"Where's the cashier?" he asked again. This time Wagley pointed to Coffman.

In addition to Coffman and Wagley, bank clerks Edith Thistlewaite and Naomi Moore had been working inside the cubicle. Several customers were forced into the small space, including Ruth Wilson. According to a contemporary article in the *Boone County Headlight*, Wilson stated that she "was rudely pushed into the cubicle."

The bandit with the rifle ignored the people filling up the small area. He moved over to Coffman. Still holding his rifle on the cashier, the robber handed him a pillow slip. "You work with me, and I'll work with you," he said.

Coffman opened the drawer, pulled out all the money, and dropped it into the sack. The bandit then shifted his gun to his left hand and ordered the cashier to go to the vault in the back of the room.

"You understand this safe better than I do," said the man with the rifle. "Open the door."

Coffman clicked several heavy knobs, then twisted the wheel. He pulled at the handle until the door sprang open. The vault was eight feet high and, in addition to containing several thousand dollars in cash, held several shelves filled with records, files, and securities.

As Coffman opened the door of the vault, bank Manager William J. Myers came toward the compartment from the rear of the bank. By now nearly a dozen employees and customers were crowded into the small space. Two robbers were trying to keep order, but there was quite a bit of milling around. J. D. Eagle, a customer, entered the bank. He was confused at seeing everyone being pushed about until someone shoved a gun barrel into his ribs and told him to go to the cubicle.

While the crowd was being held at the outer edge of the cubicle, the robber near the vault seemed to have a one-track mind. "Get in there," he ordered Myers.

The *Boone County Headlight* described what happened next:

> Mr. Myers, accepting his orders to put his hands up and 'get in there,' just walked on into the vault, the door of which was wide open. In the rear end some twenty feet back, he took down a gun [a .38-caliber Winchester rifle, model 1873] that lay upon the iron rods that tie the vault together, where it had been reposing for twelve years for just such an emergency.

Cashier Coffman, standing near the vault door, saw Myers grab the gun. Naomi Moore, still seated at her desk nearby, was also able to see into the vault. Both ducked out of the way.

The robber was about to enter the vault when Myers fired. The explosion rocked the bank, deafening those nearby.

The bandit dropped his gun, spun backward, then fell.

"Don't shoot," he cried. "Don't shoot a man who is down."

Pandemonium erupted.

Customers and employees inside the cubicle scrambled to get away, some stepping over the wounded robber. Someone picked up his rifle and placed it on a counter away from the crowd.

Myers stepped out of the vault and looked down at the robber, who lay on his back, blood soaking his suit. He seemed to be having trouble breathing.

"Will you take my glasses off?" the bandit asked.

The bank manager reached down and yanked off the cheap spectacles.

At the sound of the shot, the other outlaws panicked.

They rushed outside and scrambled into the Nash town car that had pulled up in front of the bank. As the car spun away on the icy street, Myers stepped out onto the sidewalk.

Two hundred feet away, the car approached Crooked Creek Bridge. The bank manager raised the gun to his shoulder. "Myers began pumping lead again," stated the article in the *Boone County Headlight*. "His bull's eye aim was again attested [to] by the shattered glass from the windshield that was found on the bridge. Seeing the car was getting away, he let drive at the right hind casing, which shot brought down the tire."

The car lurched away on three wheels.

Myers walked back into the bank.

"Who are you?" he asked the bandit.

"Jim McCoy," the outlaw lied.

"Who were the other men?"

"Buck Davis and Tom Jones," the robber said.

Several men helped transport the wounded robber to the doctor's office located in a tiny room above the bank. The robber moaned as he was lifted up the stairs.

He was placed on a cot in the corner of the room, surrounded by medicine bottles and surgical equipment.

Dr. T. P. Fowler examined him. The bandit was still coherent, and Fowler told him there was little that could be done. The bullet, said the doctor, had severed the man's spine, causing paralysis. Then it had passed downward and exploded his right kidney.

A crowd formed on the street outside the bank. Citizens, desperate for news, questioned anyone exiting the building.

The bandit asked Dr. Fowler if he would send for "Shorty" George Crump, a ne'er-do-well whose father, Colonel George Crump, was a well-respected merchant. The father and son soon arrived at the scene and were allowed to go upstairs.

They identified the wounded man as the infamous outlaw Henry Starr, whom they knew.

After additional medical treatment, Starr was moved to the county jail, where he asked that telegrams be sent to his family. His wife, mother, and son were soon on their way from Oklahoma to Arkansas.

The Nash was found south of town, near a railroad bridge. It had been gutted by a fire which the robbers set to throw pursuers off their tracks. Later confessions indicated that they had fled on foot through thick woods and eventually made it to Little Rock. From there they took a train back to Oklahoma.

Sheriff J. S. Johnson interviewed Starr. The cagey outlaw knew how to ingratiate himself to lawmen. He immediately gave up the names of his accomplices.

On February 18, Rufus Rowlans, identified by Starr as the outlaw who forced the bank customers into the cubicle, was arrested in Muskogee, Oklahoma. He confessed and implicated two others in the robbery. He was later convicted of the robbery and served three years in prison.

Dave Lockhart was identified as the getaway driver. A career bank robber from Searcy, Arkansas, he avoided the law for three years before he was killed in a shootout with lawmen in Tulsa, Oklahoma, in March 1924. He was suspected of participating in bank robberies in Arkansas, Missouri, and Oklahoma.

The fourth man was never caught.

Starr knew he was dying.

His mother, wife, and son arrived in town the next day.

Starr, ever the dramatist and egomaniac, issued a statement through his mother. "Send this word out to all young men for me," he said. "My advice to them is 'Don't gamble, and go straight.' See that that advice gets out, for I believe it will have importance among the young men of the country, for all are reading of my life."

The outlaw asked to speak to a reporter. "Tell Governor Robertson [who earlier had pardoned the bandit] I'm sorry that I betrayed his trust," he said. "You can't understand and probably won't believe what mental suffering I've undergone. I had every chance to go straight. I failed. I've got no defense. . . . The only excuse I have is that I was in debt. The only way I knew to get quick money was to rob a bank."

When Starr's son arrived, he lectured the boy. "Live honestly," he said. "Avoid gambling, and live within your means. And don't rob banks."

A reporter from the *Harrison Daily News* sought out Starr's mother, Mrs. Mary Gordon. "Henry has always been a trial to me," she said. "But, thank God, I will know where he is tonight. I believe his character was being moulded even before his birth. There was a serious uprising in Oklahoma in those days and those dark, dangerous days must have had a prenatal influence."

Asked if she blamed William Myers for shooting her son, Mrs. Gordon replied, "He just did what Henry would have done in his place. . . . We want him to know we don't hold it against him. If he'd shot Henry more than once, that would have been different."

It was said that Starr's last words were to his mother. "I am satisfied to die," the one-time atheist said. "I have found peace with God."

Four days after entering the First National Bank in Harrison, the notorious outlaw was dead.

He was forty-seven years old.

Starr's outlaw career spanned thirty years. More than half of those years were spent in prison. Starr was moderately successful as a bank robber. After dividing the loot from his various heists with his accomplices, he rarely came away with more than $1,000. (Contrast that with Ma Barker and her gang a few years later—they routinely scored $100,000 and more in their various robberies and kidnappings.)

There is little doubt that Starr was addicted to crime. Few criminals had as many chances to reform. Yet, like a drug addict, he kept returning to the self-destructive patterns that kept him imprisoned for much of his adult life. He could have been successful in business but couldn't stay away from his outlaw past.

William Myers had no regrets about shooting Starr. To him, it was part of the job. Indeed, eighteen years before, he'd shot another bandit who tried to rob a bank in Troy, Tennessee. For dispatching Starr, the Arkansas Bankers Association gave him a pocket watch. Script on the fob reads: "Presented to W. J. Myers. In recognition of his brave defense of the Bank of Arkansas at Harrison on February 18, 1921." He was made an honorary member of the Harrison Rotary Club.

Many people in Harrison believed that "Shorty" George Crump had helped to plan the robbery. He was known to have idolized Henry Starr, and had played cards with Dave Lockhart a few days before the robbery. However, no one ever proved that Crump had anything to do with the heist.

Relatives state that Cleve Coffman was always edgy after the robbery. He would jump at the sound of a firecracker on the Fourth of July. He once received a letter from someone in Oklahoma who asked, "What do you think of our Oklahoma bank robbers?" He replied, "If you don't want them killed, you better keep them at home."

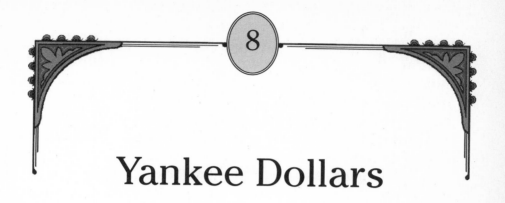

Yankee Dollars

When circumstances arose in Northfield necessitating the utmost fidelity, courage, and quick-thinking, the ordinary townsmen of a quiet Minnesota community were found ready-made for heroic stature."
— *Northfield News*, Sept. 10, 1926

The events that popularly became known as "the Great Northfield Raid" occurred on a placid autumn Tuesday in 1876. But for the invaders, the trail leading to the tranquil Minnesota farming town had begun twenty years earlier and 500 miles to the southeast.

Frank and Jesse James grew up on a farm in Clay County in western Missouri. Dr. Reuben Samuel, their stepfather, was a gentle man who farmed and practiced medicine on the side. Their mother, Zerelda, was a spitfire who doted on her sons. The boys learned to plow, furrow, hoe, and rake, and also learned the fervid Baptist interpretation of the scriptures.

The James brothers worked hard and lived comfortably in a loving, close-knit family.

Meanwhile, some forty miles south, in adjacent Jackson County, Henry Younger was providing well for his wife and twelve children. He ran a dry goods store and owned several farms, which his seven boys were dispatched to till. Like the James boys, the Younger brothers grew up accustomed to the outdoors and hard work and church on Sundays. In fact, they grew up just like other farm kids throughout America in the 1850s.

But there was a small difference. A border war was raging between Missouri and neighboring Kansas. And Clay County was in the center of its bloody path.

The purported issue was slavery. Missouri was a pro-slave state, even though few Missourians owned any. Kansas and Nebraska were territories about to become states. Eventually, the residents of the two territories would be asked to decide whether they would enter the Union as free-soil or slave. It was certain that Nebraska would come in as free-soil. If Kansas also joined as an anti-slavery state, the pro-slavery states would lose the delicate balance that its great statesmen had scratched and clawed for fifty years to maintain. The abolitionists would have the ballots in the U.S. Senate to vote slavery out of existence.

In addition to the slavery issue, the hostilities were rooted in different ways of life. Western Missouri was mostly populated by Southern farmers. They were clannish and individualistic to a fault, and would shoot people they didn't even know over an insult—real or imagined—to themselves or a kinsman.

Many Kansans were recently transplanted New Englanders, who had arrived in swarms and founded colonies throughout the territory. These newcomers were financed by the money of eastern industrialists, and their zeal was fueled by the fervid rhetoric of the religious Yankee abolitionists. Arrogant and self-righteous, they saw their Missouri neighbors as uncivilized sinners incapable of accepting the truth. Missourians perceived Kansans as aggressive meddlers out to destroy their Southern way of life.

Years before the big guns started belching at Fort Sumter, the ferocity along the Kansas-Missouri border had reached a peak unsurpassed anywhere else in America. Ruffians from both sides tried to outdo each other in sheer brutality. Burnings, lootings, and rapes were commonplace, and killings were widespread. It was against this savage backdrop that the James and Younger boys grew into manhood.

When the Civil War came to Missouri, in April of 1861, eighteen-year-old Frank James answered the call of Confederate General Sterling Price. Frank participated in the Rebel victory at Wilson's Creek on August 10, 1861, then found himself fighting the measles. Left behind by his unit to recuperate in Springfield, Frank was captured in a hospital bed when Union forces took the town. He was subsequently paroled and returned to the family farm.

By the time he was well enough to ride again, Frank found that General Price and his regular Confederate force had been pushed down to Arkansas. The Union army now controlled western Missouri. In Clay County, Frank was arrested for "suspicious conduct." He hung around the makeshift jail for a couple of weeks, then escaped.

Frank James's brief stint under General Price made him the only member of the James-Younger Gang who could claim service in a recognized regular military unit. But all of the gang's original members fought for the Confederacy.

With no options left, Frank James "went to the brush," which was a polite Missouri way of saying that someone had joined the Southern guerrillas. Their world was as dark and bloody as the black flag which served as their standard. It was a realm of night-rising, slow hangings, and continual home- and barn-burnings. There was also a concept the Jameses and Youngers would remember much later and draw upon: the notion of town-taking.

In the summer of 1862, Frank James joined the "bushwhackers," as William Clarke Quantrill's raiders were called by those with pro-Union sympathies. Cole Younger was already there.

The Missouri guerrillas were, simply put, the most blood-thirsty mounted regiments in the war. They were led by Quantrill. Two of his chieftains, George Todd and "Bloody" Bill Anderson, later split off and founded their own outfits. After the breakup, the bands occasionally rode together to fight a common enemy. Their most hated opponents were the Kansas Jayhawkers, headed by Doc Jennison, and the Kansas Redlegs, led by Jim Lane. These Kansas guerrilla forces killed, robbed, and generally terrorized anyone who seemed to show a preference for the Confederacy.

Brutality, arson, and murder were common, and a strike by one side inevitably sparked retaliation by the other. After a particularly successful Quantrill assault, the Union command ordered that all captured guerrillas be hanged as murderers, instead of treated as prisoners of war. Quantrill, of course, announced that he would respond in kind.

Quantrill was unschooled in military strategy, but it quickly became clear that he had an eye for the game. Even his critics concede that he was an excellent tactician. As the most hunted individual on the border, it seems incredible that he managed to stay at large and do the Union substantial damage until the waning days of the war.

Quantrill's most memorable victory was the sacking of Lawrence, Kansas. The guerrillas rode in with 750 men and a hit list about a mile long. Participating in this mission were Frank James and Cole Younger—and a seventeen-year-old baby-faced killer named Jesse James. When the guerrillas left, 200 Lawrence men lay dead, and the town was nothing but three square miles of hot ashes.

Quantrill was the first recorded Civil War leader to declare the sword obsolete. He laughed at the romanticized saber, preferring pistols. Their bullets reached farther than a saber and hit with a shock that was final. Add to that the fact that you have five bullets—the hammer being down on an empty chamber—to get you through it all. Unless, of course, you carried more than one pistol.

The Texas Rangers had been fighting this way since 1852. Quantrill, like the Rangers, preferred the .44-caliber Colt Navy model. But Quantrill pushed this strategy a step farther, having each of his men carry at least three revolvers during a charge. This lesson would not be forgotten by the Jameses and the Youngers.

Frank James and Cole Younger rode with Quantrill throughout the war. Jesse and Jim Younger entered the war late because of their ages, but what Jesse lacked in experience he compensated for in ruthlessness. Jesse found his way into Bloody Bill Anderson's unit and quickly made a name for himself. "For a beardless boy," said Bloody Bill, "he is the best fighter in the command."

This was no small praise, considering Anderson was probably the most venomous killer in the entire war. He carried eight Colts in his belt during combat, and four more in his saddlebags. Bloody Bill's bridle was adorned with dried human ears, and his saddle horn always toted a multitude of Yankee scalps. One of his sisters had been raped by the Redlegs, and another had died while in Union custody. Anderson asked no quarter from his enemies, and he emphatically gave none.

In the summer of '64, Jesse was shot through the lung during a raid at Heisinger's Lake. He very nearly died but was back in the saddle by the middle of September.

He was present when Anderson's outfit took the town of Centralia, Missouri, which had a small Union force guarding it. The garrison fled, and Anderson's men were partaking of the town's liquor supply when a train chugged in. On board were twenty-five Union soldiers, unarmed and going home on leave. The guerrillas pulled them off the train and lined them up. The one survivor, who was shot between the eyes but didn't die, later testified that Bloody Bill had shot all of the bluecoats himself, while his men kept them covered.

The tides of war begin to turn shortly after Centralia. Of the notorious guerrilla leaders, George Todd was the first to go. On September 23, Todd took a rifle ball in the neck during a raid near Sugar Creek, Missouri. Jesse James was one of the mourners at his grave.

Bloody Bill's luck ran out near the end of October at the town of Orrick, Missouri. He rode blind into a Union ambush and was perforated before he could draw one of his many Navy-model Colts.

William Clarke Quantrill was the canniest of the Southern guerrilla chieftains—and the most civilized. For him, the curtain closed on New Year's Day, 1865, near Louisville, Kentucky. He was scouting alone when he ran head-on into a group of Kansas Redlegs. He turned his horse and raced for safety, but a ball from a Spencer cut him down.

A few months later, in the parlor of a home in Appomattox Court House, Virginia, the Confederate dream died. Already dead were George Todd, Bill Anderson, and Quantrill. But a lot of men who had ridden with them were not.

On July 26, 1865, Frank James cantered into Samuel's Depot, Kentucky, and declared his fealty to the Union. Promptly paroled, he traveled west to the family farm.

Cole Younger, with a reputation among sharpshooters as an unerring marksman, was also one of the more restrained members of Quantrill's band. It is well-documented that he braved Bloody Bill himself to save the life of a wounded Union colonel that Anderson was preparing to scalp. After the surrender, word was sent out to the Union garrisons in Missouri and Kentucky to make Cole Younger's surrender as painless and honorable as possible. Instead, Cole hot-footed it to Scyene, Texas, without surrendering at all. He'd wintered in Scyene with Quantrill's men during the war, and it was there that he'd fathered Myra Maybelle Shirley's first child. Myra later became famous as Belle Starr.

Jim Younger finally was allowed by Cole to join the army when Jim turned sixteen. He served with his brother under Quantrill and saw some furious fighting in the short time he was with the unit. Jim was around the farmyard near Louisville when Quantrill was shot, and he was nabbed by regular Union forces in the dragnet thrown out after the dying Quantrill was identified. Jim Younger finished the war in a federal prison in Illinois. He was paroled from there when the war ended and returned to Jackson County.

For Jesse James, surrendering was a little harder. He and some cohorts were riding into Lexington, Missouri, to lay down their arms when they ran into a detachment of the Second Wisconsin Cavalry. Jesse was shot in the chest despite the white flag that his unit was riding under. He was rushed to a hospital and treated. The Union commander at Lexington, a Major Rogers, waived the oath-taking and wrote in a report that the young Rebel "will soon be surrendering to a higher authority than mine." Jesse convalesced in the hospital until he was well enough to travel, then found his way back home to recover.

One day in January 1866, John Younger and twelve-year-old Bob drove their mother to Independence to obtain their monthly supplies. While shopping, a vagrant named Gilcreas made some disparaging remarks about Cole, who still hadn't returned from the war. Fifteen-year-old Jim then made some disparaging remarks about Gilcreas. The older man responded by smacking John in the face with a frozen fish. John promptly shot his assailant between the eyes with one of Cole's pistols. A slingshot was found in the hip pocket of the deceased, and a pro-Southern coroner's jury ruled that Younger had fired in self-defense. But incidents of this sort were piling up, and the Younger family was beginning to feel a bit uneasy. They felt a little better, though, a few days later when Cole finally showed up.

In late January 1866, Cole Younger rode over to Clay County to visit with his old friend and companion Frank

James. While there, Cole was introduced by Frank to his ailing brother, Jesse.

In early February, Jim Younger returned to the family farm in Jackson County. Almost simultaneously, several banks within a 200-mile radius of Clay County were robbed in broad daylight.

On a Tuesday afternoon in mid-February, several men rode into the square at Liberty, Missouri. Two went into the Clay County Savings Bank. They emerged a couple of minutes later with a sack containing $60,000 worth of bearer bonds and paper money. A student from William Jewell College was standing on the sidewalk across the street watching the activity. He was gunned down by a mounted raider, for reasons known only to the shooter, and later died from his wound. The bank was forced to settle with its depositors for fifty cents on the dollar, then closed its doors.

The audacious stickup was the first peacetime daylight bank robbery ever recorded. But it assuredly would not be the last. Nobody has ever made an iron-clad case against any of the participants. Every credible theory, however, points to Frank James and Cole Younger as being involved. Conversely, Jesse James was still an invalid when the robbery transpired and almost certainly was not a part of it. Jim Younger may have been there, but some persuasive evidence puts him out of the area at the time. At any rate, Cole Younger was known to have cashed bearer bonds for several years.

The next robbery was May 22, 1867, at the Hughes & Wasson Bank in Richmond, Missouri. Ten men participated. The take was $4,000. Some townsmen fought back, and the mayor of the town was killed. Then the robbers attacked the local jail, trying to free some ex-Confederate guerrillas who were locked up on various charges. The jailer and his son resisted and were promptly slain. The robbers rode away untouched. (The reporter for the local newspaper was so outraged at the murders of local citizens that he failed to mention whether the breakout was successful.)

In March 1868, the gang struck again. The Long Banking Company in Russellville, Kentucky, was robbed of $14,000. Nobody was killed in this holdup, but it was quite evident that robbing banks was becoming a popular pastime in that neck of the woods.

Cole Younger apparently decided to take a leave of absence from his occupation of choice.

Some historians have speculated that it was Cole and Jim's share of the loot that financed the Youngers' relocation to Texas. Cole had some fond memories of the Lone Star State, and in autumn of 1868 he loaded up his long-suffering mother, Bursheba, and all her worldly possessions and headed south. Jim, John, and Bob accompanied them.

But back in Missouri, the James boys were still doing business. They hit the only bank in Gallatin, Missouri, on December 12, 1868. Jesse shot the cashier, because he was slow handing over the cash. The bank president, former Union Captain John Sheets, was shot for no apparent reason, and a bank customer and a local attorney were also wounded. Sheets later died, and whispered names began to circulate. There were many rumor-mills, and many names made the rounds, but three were uttered by almost every speculator: Frank James, Jesse James, and McClelland Miller.

Clel Miller was a Clay County resident who had ridden with Bloody Bill Anderson. There he almost certainly met Jesse James, if he didn't already know him. Miller was trusted by both the James boys and the Younger clan and was present at every robbery pulled off by the gang.

Meanwhile, down in Texas, the fire was going out between Cole and Myra Shirley. He might have been getting restless, or the family may have worn out its welcome. In the winter of 1870, John Younger was named in a misdemeanor disorderly conduct charge. When two of the town deputies came to arrest him, John went for his gun. A shootout ensued. When the black powder smoke had cleared, one deputy lay dead, the other was mortally wounded, and John was standing upright with a hole through his arm. He immediately fled across the state line into Arkansas, then moved up to Kansas City.

Cole, meanwhile, allegedly had impregnated Myra Shirley and certainly had returned to Missouri.

In June 1871, the James-Younger members pulled off the easiest bank job of their careers. The town was Corydon, Iowa, and a famous public speaker, Henry Clay Dean, had come to deliver an oration. That afternoon, he was well into his second hour. His podium was on a shady hill about a mile outside of town when four men on horseback pulled up on the outskirts of the crowd. At one of the horsemen's signaled request, Dean suspended the flow of golden words from his silver tongue.

"I yield to the gentleman on horseback," he generously obliged.

"Uh, your bank's just been robbed," Cole Younger is reported to have drawled, "and maybe somebody ought to go untie the cashier."

The robbers were Frank and Jesse James, Cole Younger, and Clel Miller, and they were identified in print by the *Kansas City Times*. Jesse fired a vehement denial back at the *Times*, which was printed. But the newspaper stood by its accusations. Clel Miller was later arrested and charged, but he produced witnesses who swore that he had been in Missouri at the time of the robbery. Miller was acquitted.

Cole now settled back in Missouri and refocused his energies on his outlaw calling. He invited Jim and John to stand by to join the gang if called on. Jim reluctantly agreed, while John eagerly assented.

But the new members weren't used on the next job. It was in April 1872 and the place was Columbia, Kentucky. Two men burst into the bank as two sat horseback outside the door. It was crowded inside. The cashier yelled a warning when he saw the drawn pistols of the strangers. He was instantly shot, and a general panic erupted. Patrons dove through windows and crawled out doors as Jesse James scooped up $600 and beat a hasty exit.

As a robbery, Columbia was a fizzle. It also sparked the first round in a protracted conflict that would last until Jesse James drew his last breath.

The Pinkerton National Detective Agency was the largest detective agency in the world in the mid-1800s. In addition to investigating crimes, the agency also pursued individual criminals and outlaw gangs, as well as providing security on railroad trains in an effort to prevent robberies. Its most well-heeled clients were the banks, which collectively retained Pinkerton services. Pinkerton agents were rigorously screened for intelligence and honesty before employment was offered. Their operatives, on the other hand, were mostly Civil War veterans from both sides who could shoot, ride, and generally survive the harsh elements and the hard men who lived in them.

A Pinkerton agent with a provocative nickname, Yankee Bligh, identified Cole, Frank, and Jesse as three of the Columbia stickup men.

In the fall of 1872, three men held up the Kansas City Exposition. One robber grabbed the money box, removed the cash, and stuck it into his pocket. The attendant grappled with the robber, whose accomplice cranked off a round at the aggressive cashier. The bullet missed but hit a little girl who was visiting the fair with her mother. The robbers got lost in the crowd, but not before one of them dramatically announced to the spectators that he was Jesse James.

Jesse frequently wrote letters to newspaper editors denying his involvement in any crimes. His favorite newspaper was the *Osceola Democrat*, and his favorite publisher was John Newman Edwards, who owned a string of weeklies. He had been a champion of the Confederate cause and, in the 1870s, was a very vocal guardian of all its veterans.

After the Kansas City caper, Jesse was taking some heat about his choices of targets and the marksmanship of his followers. He quickly fired off a letter to Edwards refuting his participation, then went on to deny that Frank James and Cole Younger were involved either. The usually easy-going Younger was infuriated, since he hadn't been considered a suspect until Jesse's written denial. Legend holds that he went stalking after Jesse and might have killed him if the always level-headed Frank hadn't intervened.

Jim Younger returned to Texas in the winter of 1872. Incredibly, he became a police officer in Dallas. He lasted until February of 1873 when he and a fellow officer were indicted for robbery. Shortly after posting bond, Jim became the second Younger to flee the Lone Star state.

In Missouri, Cole recruited his brother John to help rob the Ste. Genevieve Savings Bank. The take was $4,000, and this time nobody got hurt.

While the Civil War raged in the winter of 1862, two brothers had successfully robbed a train. Jesse and Cole had been too busy at the time to take note of this peculiar incident, but others had. And so, in June of 1873, someone mentioned that railway express cars sometimes carried lots of cash. After that it was just a matter of choosing which train to rob.

The gang assembled in Adair, Iowa. Present were Frank and Jesse, along with Cole, Jim, John, and Bob Younger. Two newcomers joined the group: Bill Chadwell, a friend of Jesse from his guerrilla days, and Charlie Pitts, a friend of Cole. Clel Miller rounded out the crew.

The target was a Rock Island express train headed for Chicago. Near a spot known as Turkey Creek, the gang pried a rail loose and waited. The *Rock Island Special* came along on schedule and derailed in a cloud of smoke and flames. The engineer was killed, along with several passengers. The take was a measly $3,000, along with a thousand or so taken from the passengers. But it created further notoriety for the gang.

Afterward, Jesse wrote his obligatory letter of denial, omitting any reference to Cole Younger. Jim, the most sensitive member of the gang, suffered a bout of remorse about those who had been killed. He refused to accept any of the money and announced that he was through robbing folks.

Area railroad companies formed an association similar to the one the midwestern bankers had already established. The railroad association also followed the lead of the bankers and retained the Pinkerton National Detective Agency to follow the James-Younger Gang to the ends of the earth, if need be. But bring them to justice, dead or alive.

The gang hit another train, this time in a small Missouri town near St. Louis in a place called Gad's Hill. This one was bloodless. The robbers simply went aboard when the train stopped for coal. The participants were the James brothers, the Younger brothers minus Jim, and Clel Miller. They got away clean, then disbanded and spread out over five states.

The written publicity about the gang, subdued until Turkey Creek, accelerated to a crescendo. Even the *St. Louis Dispatch*, the cornerstone of John Edwards's empire, identified the perpetrators by name. Edwards, who was out of state at the time, hurried home to print a retraction.

Pinkerton, which had lucrative contracts with both the bankers and the railroads, decided to take the offensive against the James-Younger Gang. The opening salvo was a fizzle. An operative named Whicher rode up to the Jameses' Clay County farm and announced that he was seeking work as a farmhand. That area of Missouri probably harbored the most suspicious population—outlaws and decent inhabitants—in the entire United States. The next thing heard regarding Mr. Whicher was when he turned up dead with a chest full of bullets. The press speculated that Jesse James did the killing. Frank was thought to be in Tennessee at the time.

In March 1874, a Pinkerton operative and a Missouri peace officer showed up in Jackson County announcing that

131

they were looking to buy cattle. Jim took John with him and went looking for them. The two parties met up on a deserted road. A mounted shootout followed. The Pinkerton man, the lawman, and John Younger were mortally wounded. Jim waited around until his brother was properly buried, then departed for California to work on his Uncle Coleman's small ranch.

Bob Younger, agonizing in the afterthoughts of his venture into high-profile robbery, sought out his sisters in Denison, Texas. Jesse finally married his childhood sweetheart and first cousin, Zerelda "Zee" Mimms, and they left for Texas.

By December 1874, the gang was back in the Midwest. Frank and Jesse, Cole and Bob, and Clel Miller held up a Kansas Pacific train near the small town of Muncie, Kansas. This time their proceeds were more than $30,000.

Afterward, Cole and Bob hid out in Indian Territory, and the James brothers went with them. They stayed at the outlaw sanctuary operated by Tom Starr, the first father-in-law of Myra Shirley. His lair was deep in the big bend in the Canadian River, and Starr ran a rudimentary safe-haven resort for the most wanted fugitives in Arkansas and Oklahoma. The site was hidden back in the most sinister site on that treacherous river, impossible to find without a guide. When the gang left, Myra named it Younger's Bend.

Then on January 27, 1875, a sordid incident of such low proportions that even Frank and Jesse probably wouldn't have stooped to was executed by the Pinkertons. Hoping that Jesse and Frank were inside the Samuels' farmhouse, twenty-two Pinkerton agents surrounded it. When no one came out at their command, the Pinkertons lofted two incindiary devices into the house. They intended to burn down the farmhouse—and Frank and Jesse, too—but the outlaws weren't there. An explosion ensued in which mother Zerelda lost an arm and a younger half-brother was killed.

The response from law-abiding Missourians was fast, furious, and fervent. Predictably, Edwards, publisher of the *St. Louis Dispatch*, waved the bloody flag in a hydrophobic editorial:

> Men of Missouri, you who fought under Anderson, Quantrill, Todd . . . recall your woodscraft and give up these scoundrels to the Henry rifle and the Colt's revolver. It is because, like you, they were at Lawrence and Centralia . . . and wherever else the black flag floated.

Suddenly, the eyes of ordinary people—people who had disapproved of the Jameses and the Youngers—were focused right on the Pinkerton agency. Even the pro-Union factions in Missouri thought the private cops had overreached the boundaries of proper manhunting.

The hullabaloo became so great that the authorities had to act. In March 1875, a grand jury returned indictments for murder against several operatives and Allan Pinkerton himself, the detective agency's founder and president. Pinkerton coughed up some big bucks and brought in a bevy of famous lawyers. Then the wheels of justice ground to a halt.

At this time, Frank James was raising horses in Nashville, Tennessee, and living the tranquil life of a Southern gentleman with his new bride. Jesse, however, had returned to Clay County as soon as he heard about the bombing. He set to work immediately. A bit of investigating turned up the fact that one of the Pinkerton men indicted by the grand jury had worked as a hired hand for a neighbor of the Samuels. Shortly afterward, Daniel Askew, the neighbor, walked out on his porch and was shot through the chest by an unseen assailant. It's still unclear whether Askew was acting in collusion with the Pinkertons or was just an over-worked farmer who had hired himself some help.

About the same time, the spring of 1875, there was a move in the Tennessee legislature to grant amnesty to the James brothers and Cole and Jim Younger. The bill almost passed, falling just two votes shy of the two-thirds majority required for approval. The sponsors vowed to try again during the General Assembly's next session, and the chance of passage looked promising.

Except that the outlaw gang just couldn't stop robbing banks. Jesse was too hot for Frank and Cole after the murder of Askew, but Frank needed more money to maintain the standard of Southern gentility that he'd assumed in Nashville. So he hunted up Cole and, with two newcomers, robbed a bank in Huntington, West Virginia. One of the new men was killed and the other was captured, but Frank and Cole got away. Jesse, of course, fired off the usual letter to the press protesting his innocence—but this time he was telling the truth.

However, Jesse had been contemplating an idea that had dawned on him a month earlier while chewing the fat with Bill Chadwell, so this denial wasn't as vigorous as his earlier ones had been.

Bill Chadwell was a short, scrawny windbag born and bred in Minnesota's rich farming country. He'd done farm chores and odd jobs around Clay County for several years, and Jesse was convinced that he wasn't a Pinkerton man. Chadwell chattered incessantly, so much so that he'd earned the nickname "Windy Bill" from those who had to listen to him.

What Chadwell had talked to Jesse about was distant banks, unprotected and brimming with money deposited by prosperous farmers and merchants. Jesse had studied the idea long and hard. A lucrative strike would permit him to take Zee and the children and move out of the firing line forever. He particularly liked the idea of going to California.

But there was a difficulty that he would have to surmount in order to put his plan into action. His brother,

Frank, thought Chadwell was a fraud, and Cole Younger saw him as a lunatic and a liar. Jesse would need to neutralize the opinions of those two strong-willed henchmen.

To do so Jesse met with Bob Younger in a Kansas City hotel. He and Bob had become close friends back when Jesse and Zee honeymooned down in Texas. Jesse laid out the plan, naming Mankato, Minnesota, as a possible target. He never mentioned Chadwell's name. After two days of deliberation, Jesse sent Bob Younger off to enlist Cole for the mission. Then Jesse went to persuade Frank to join up.

It was easy to persuade Frank, since he always needed money to maintain his image as a successful breeder of horses. But Cole was a hard sell.

When Bob broached the subject, Cole Younger reportedly went through the ceiling. He immediately suspected Bill Chadwell to be the instigator, and he opposed working so far from home. But Bob believed in Jesse, and Jesse had never guessed wrong. So Bob argued, and Cole objected, and finally Bob wore his older brother down. Or at least that's what Cole says in his autobiography, *The Story of Cole Younger, by Himself.*

After all was said and done, Cole cabled Jim in California, where Jim was living a law-abiding—if unexciting—life as a cowboy. "Come home. Bob needs you" was the simple message, and Jim headed back to Missouri. Much later, he said he returned because he thought Bob was in some kind of trouble.

With the nucleus of his gang back in Clay County and eager to get on with the robbery, Jesse convened a strategy session.

Also present was the ubiquitous Clel Miller. At the meeting Jesse pointed out that the operation would be expensive—so acquiring some seed money was imperative. There would be train fare north, plus cash for hotels and meals. And, of course, they would need some of the finest horseflesh in Minnesota in order to get back to Missouri in one piece.

135

What Jesse was pointing out was that the gang would have to commit a local robbery to finance a distant one. It was decided then that they would rob a Missouri-Pacific train at a railroad construction site near Otterville, Missouri. Jim Younger, still suffering remorse over the death of the engineer on the *Rock Island Special*, simply said he wasn't going to rob any more trains, so an amateur stand-in, Hobbs Kerry, was recruited.

The train robbery went down without a hitch. The bandits captured a flagman, whose lantern they used to stop the train. Then they simply boarded it, ransacked the safe, and crammed $15,000 into a gunnysack. About $1,000 more was taken from the passengers. However, the robbers announced that they would not take one red cent from anyone who had fought for the Confederacy. The outlaws were customarily courteous to women passengers, and they took nothing from them this time, either.

The capital for the raid into Minnesota was in the gang's pockets. The only problem was Hobbs Kerry. He went on a spending spree in his hometown in southern Missouri and quickly found himself arrested. A petty thief whose typical harvest was a hog or a few chickens, Kerry's spending of wads of folding money caught the eye of the local lawmen. After a few threats and a little muscle, Kerry began to sing like a bird. He sang again the next day for reporters, Pinkerton agents, and railroad detectives, naming everyone who who had participated in the Missouri-Pacific robbery.

Jesse once again saw his name in headlines. And once again he responded in print. Jesse lambasted Hobbs Kerry as a notorious liar and "paltroon" and offered to produce an alibi with a hundred witnesses. He went on to blame the man who had led the posse out Sedalia, one Bacon Montgomery. As for letters to the editors go, it was probably Jesse's magnum opus.

Privately, Jesse was agitated. The amnesty, which had seemed almost a sure thing a week before, was going up in smoke. The manhunters—Pinkerton agents and railroad detectives—would be pressing the attorney general to indict the men named by Hobbs Kerry. And worse, public opinion might turn around on the gang.

Jesse and Frank James, with Cole Younger, deliberated for a few days and decided it was time to travel north. They didn't fear what was behind them, and they were confident of what was ahead. The word went out, the invited men assembled at Monagaw Cave, and the James–Younger Gang left Missouri to hunt out a fat, unprotected bank in nonviolent Minnesota.

After the raid in Corydon, Iowa, five years earlier, Cole Younger had been widely quoted as saying, "We are rough men used to rough ways." Absolutely. They fought the guerrilla way, and both Jameses and Cole Younger had been praised by their respective leaders as being among the best in the elite companies of horse soldiers. They were highly mobile, utterly ruthless, and splendid horsemen. *The Kansas City Star* said this about them after the Northfield raid:

> The Jameses and Youngers were always painstaking in their preparations. It is a known fact that these men, when in tight places, would take the bridle reins in their teeth, guide their horses by a touch of the knee or a touch of the rein on his neck, while using a gun in both hands as they rode at breakneck speed.

The Jameses and the Youngers had lived off the land while being chased through the backwoods of five states in which they had robbed and killed. They had been trained from manhood to perform their chosen occupation, and they were more than competent at it. They were the best at what they did, they knew it, and they were eager to get to Minnesota.

The Undine region of southern Minnesota is a farmer's paradise. The soil is rich and black, the streams are abundant, and lakes are plentiful. First surveyed for the War Department in the late 1830s, the virgin land was ripe for settlement. The surveyor had some hearty praise for the valley, and when his report was published, the New England Yankees and the Swedes and Norwegians who read it knew what to do to turn the prairie into farmland.

These settlers came from different places with different cultures, but they all possessed a strong work ethic and a belief in the concept of law and order. Communities sprang up along the Cannon River and its tributaries, and one of these was Northfield. There, all of the newcomers seemed to hold the same basic core values as the pioneers. The men were up at dawn and farmed until sundown, with church on Sundays. There was no law enforcement to speak of, because there wasn't any crime. All of the men owned rifles for hunting, but any handguns seen around the community were carried by strangers.

But while the Northfield men were peaceful, they were far from faint-hearted. During the Civil War, at least 800 Rice County men had served in the Second, Fourth, Sixth, and Eighth Minnesota Volunteer Infantry. And seventy had served in one of the most heroic regiments in the entire Union Army—the First Minnesota Volunteers. G Company of that most-decorated regiment was composed entirely of Northfield men. A ferocious bayonet charge on the second day at Gettysburg saved the Union's exposed flank. But it cost the First Minnesota 82 percent of its men, the highest casualty rate suffered by any unit in an engagement during the war. The Northfield men might have traded their swords for plowshares after the war ended, but they were some very tough individuals indeed.

The main crop in Rice County wasn't rice, but wheat, and by 1866 there were more than 800 farms that were producing it. A sailor turned miller, Jesse Ames, was grinding out 150 barrels of flower every twenty-four hours, but that production rate wasn't what put Northfield on the map. Ames had a special method for refining the wheat as it was being ground, and the result was a delicious variety known as Northfield flour. It was famous throughout the Midwest and commanded a higher price per barrel. Jesse Ames became so successful that he branched out into other endeavors. In 1876, he was vice president of the First National Bank of Northfield.

Industry soon followed the farmers. By 1876, the town boasted a steel mill, a plow factory, and some cooperage shops which produced barrels for Northfield flour. There were also blacksmith shops and a fledgling brick factory. It seemed there was a job for anybody in Northfield who wanted to work.

The layout of the town in 1876 was visionary and symmetrical. Back then, one rode into Northfield over the Cannon River Bridge. Division Street, in the center of town, was the main thoroughfare, and businesses lined both sides of the street. Near the town square two hardware stores sat side by side, and next to them was a stone office building named the Scriver Building. Across the street was a two-story wooden building which housed the *Rice County Journal*, a newspaper that hit the streets every Thursday. Across the square on the right side was the entrance to the First National Bank.

Housed in the Scriver Building, the First National Bank was founded in 1876, the result of the merger of two private banks. The site was to be a temporary one, and already First National was seeking permanent quarters. It had no bars or grills, and the counter was low enough to climb over.

The vault, though, was imposing. It was state of the art for the time, made by the Detroit Safe Company. Inside was 6,500 pounds of iron made by the Philadelphia firm of Evans

& Watson. It featured a Yale time lock that was a prototype of that prestigious locksmithing firm.

The front door and two windows of the bank opened onto Division Street, which was the busiest street in the town. A third window and a back door opened into an alley. Across the alley was Manning's Hardware.

Working inside the bank was Joseph Lee Heywood, age thirty-nine, the bookkeeper and assistant cashier. A Union Army veteran, Heywood had worked at First National since 1872. He also served as treasurer for the city of Northfield and was the comptroller of Carleton College. Heywood's assistant was Alonzo Bunker, a New Hampshire native and part-time student at Carleton. The third employee on duty that day was a local man, a temporary cashier named Frank Wilcox.

The James-Younger Gang began filtering into Minnesota in mid-August. This time the members were Jesse and his brother Frank; Cole, Jim, and Bob Younger; Charlie Pitts; Bill Chadwell; and, of course, Clel Miller.

They arrived on trains, in groups of twos and threes, and began surveying the townships throughout the Cannon River Valley while shopping for suitable horses. All eight of the gang members stayed at the Nicollette House, the finest hotel in Minneapolis, for two nights. But the hotel manager apparently became suspicious of the eight hard-looking men with Southern accents, and he assigned the hotel detective to keep on eye on them, which he did. During their stay, Chadwell—also known as Bill Stiles—was walking with five cohorts when he ran into a peace officer who had once arrested him for stealing a horse. Chadwell told the policeman that he was doing well and planning to travel to the Black Hills and prospect for gold. The next day the gang crossed the Mississippi and entered the town of Red Wing, Minnesota.

In Red Wing, most of the gang stayed at the National Hotel, where they posed as cattle buyers. While there, they bought four horses. But Frank and Jesse went down to Brush Prairie, near Northfield, passing themselves off as investors looking to buy some farmland.

All eight members of the crew met in Mankato on the first day of September. Most accounts hold that they intended to rob the bank that day but were deterred by a large crowd gathered near it. They reportedly split up and rode off in three directions. But the word had been given, and the gang was to convene at the Cannon River Bridge in Northfield on September 7, 1876. Across that structure they would ride into immortality and put the small town on the national map.

It was a warm Indian summer afternoon when eight long riders entered the town from the west. They all wore linen dusters, and they weren't concerned about being inconspicuous. With four or five Colt Navy revolvers bulging beneath each jacket, they split into three units. The first group was composed of Frank James, Bob Younger, and Charlie Pitts. They rode side by side across the Cannon River Bridge, crossed the square, and hitched their horses in front of the bank. Drawing suspicious looks from several pedestrians, the trio sat down on some boxes in front of a dry goods store and tried to act nonchalant. But it seems that every passerby in sight cast wary glances at them. Then Cole Younger and Clel Miller came riding over the bridge, and a few townspeople made a beeline for the bank to warn the employees that a robbery might soon be in progress.

At least a hundred citizens were milling around on Division Street, and while some of them believed they would soon be witnessing a bank robbery, most didn't. Prairie chicken season had just started, and some citizens believed that the heavily armed strangers were hunters. Others thought that the hard-eyed riders were part of a Wild West show scheduled to perform that night. A few even thought they were just drunken cowmen celebrating a successful buy or a successful sale.

Finally, the last three outlaws showed up. Jesse, Jim Younger, and Bill Chadwell rode over the bridge and pulled up. The plan called for them to charge down Division Street amid gunsmoke and Rebel yells if the bank robbery went sour. In essence, they would be a covering force if the men in the bank had to retreat.

J. S. "Sim" Allen owned a hardware store just west of the bank. He saw the three outlaws outside the dry goods store get off their boxes and step into the bank and correctly assumed that the strangers were going inside to rob it. He started walking toward the bank. Clel Miller saw him and dismounted. Miller grabbed Allen by the collar, bellowed a string of obscenities, and stuck a revolver in front of Allen's nose. Allen struggled, and Miller fired two rounds.

With the first gunshot, the three raiders who had been waiting near the bridge charged down Division Street firing their revolvers and shouting expletives. Allen tore himself from Miller's grasp and sprinted toward his hardware store, screaming that the bank was being robbed. Several onlookers took to their heels and followed Allen. Others ducked behind any object they could find.

Cole and Clel Miller jumped up on their mounts as Jesse, Jim Younger, and Chadwell galloped up to the bank. Gun smoke clouded Division Street as Northfield's church bells began to ring the alarm.

Things were getting bad outside the bank, but they were already dismal inside it. Despite the attempts of townspeople to warn the bankers, nobody had made it inside; thus, the cashier, Heywood, and his two assistants were taken completely by surprise.

Frank, Bob Younger, and Pitts entered the bank with drawn revolvers, warning that forty men were outside who would raze the town unless the bank employees came up with a substantial amount of cash.

In one of his many interviews granted afterward, assistant cashier Bunker recalled, "Those revolvers were pointed at our faces, and the hole in each of them seemed about as large as a hat. I was commanded to throw up my hands. Under the circumstances, this seemed the most appropriate thing to do, and I threw them up."

Bookkeeper Wilcox remembered most vividly that the robbers were dead serious. "Throw up your hands," he quoted Frank James as saying, "And if you holler, we will blow your brains out." Wilcox added that he could think of nothing to do but comply.

J. L. Heywood was sitting at the cashier's desk. As the oldest man present, he was soon singled out by Frank James.

"Are you the cashier?" James demanded.

"No," Heywood replied.

But James was having none of it.

"You're the cashier!" he roared. "Now open the safe, you son of a bitch!"

The vault was already open, and a robber saw it and stepped inside. According to Wilcox, Heywood sprang forward and slammed the door shut. But it didn't lock. Wilcox described the incarcerated robber as "a slim, dark-complexioned man with a black mustache." Bob Younger turned the vault handle, and out stepped Charlie Pitts.

Now Frank James and Pitts were infuriated. They dragged Heywood back from the safe, and Pitts slapped him a few times. Again, they commanded him to open the safe. Heywood calmly told the robbers that he couldn't open it, because the safe was controlled by a time lock.

Charlie Pitts began to beat Heywood in the face.

"Murder!" screamed the cashier. "Murder!"

He was promptly rewarded with a crushing blow from a revolver to his forehead. He crumpled and fell behind his desk, unmoving.

Pitts pulled a massive Bowie knife from his boot and cut the hapless Heywood across the throat. Frank James and Bob Younger dragged the semiconscious cashier into the vault and threatened him with instantaneous death if he didn't unlock the safe.

Actually, the safe was closed and latched, but it wasn't locked. According to standard banking practices of the day, the combination dial had not been turned. Anyone could have pulled the door open with a finger, but Heywood and his assistants bravely refused to tell the outlaws. There was about $12,000 in the safe and another $3,000 spread out in counter trays. The $15,000 in the First National Bank that day was less than the seed money the outlaws had taken from the Missouri-Pacific train to finance the trip north.

Bob Younger moved across the room to guard the two junior employees and search for loose cash. He forced Wilcox to kneel as he vainly ransacked some cash drawers. While his head was turned, Bunker jumped to his feet and dashed toward the back door. Pitts saw him, shouted, and fired a pistol ball past Bunker's ear. Bunker burst through the unlocked back door and started running across the alley toward Manning's Hardware. Pitts came out the back door and fired two more rounds. The second shot went through Bunker's right shoulder. Bunker staggered, then changed his destination to a doctor's office a block away.

Outside, Cole Younger was shouting for his cohorts in the bank to come on out.

"The game is up!" he is widely quoted as saying. "Better get out, boys. They're killing all our men!"

The sounds of gunfire were growing louder and more frequent. Bob Younger came out of the bank and mounted his horse. Cole Younger dismounted and ran to the bank.

"For God's sake," he shouted, "Come out!"

With no money to show for their efforts, Frank James and Charlie Pitts backed out of the bank. As they started out the door, Heywood staggered to his feet and reeled across the room.

Frank James took deliberate aim and shot him between the eyes.

While Heywood was being battered inside the bank, Henry Wheeler, a University of Michigan medical student home for the holiday, was about to turn warrior. He ran first to his father's drugstore to get his rifle but remembered that he'd left it at home. Next, he ran over to the Dampier Hotel, where he found an old single-shot Sharps rifle. Wheeler rummaged around and found four cartridges, which he took and then scurried up the stairs to the third floor. There he knocked out a window pane and began surveying the street down below.

At the same time, Sim Allen was in his hardware store handing out rifles to anybody who would take one. Next door, A. R. Manning picked up a single-shot Winchester from his hardware store. Grabbing some loose shells, he headed for the corner where Scriver Avenue met Division Street. By the time he got there, hell had already broken loose.

Four outlaws were riding back and forth along Division, howling, cursing, and continually firing their weapons. While most residents sought cover, some did not.

E. S. Bill came out of the Shatto store where he and his wife had been shopping. Brandishing a long-barreled revolver, he stood in front of the large glass window looking for a target. An outlaw saw him and snapped off a shot, shattering the window. Nothing more was heard from Bill.

A few of the people in town that day were carrying shotguns, but they were loaded with birdshot meant for prairie chickens. Nonetheless, a clerk in Allen's hardware store discharged his shotgun into Clel Miller's face at a distance of about ten yards. The blast knocked Miller off his horse, but the robber was able to climb back on. Manning was looking for targets, but when he couldn't get a bead on an outlaw, he shot a tethered horse he didn't recognize. But when he worked the bolt of the Winchester, nothing happened. The cartridge had jammed in the chamber, and he couldn't work it out. So off he ran to his hardware store to find a ramrod to dislodge the shell casing.

Manning returned to the corner to find a mounted man between the horses and bank door. He fired hurriedly, and the bullet glanced off a wooden hitching post and slammed into Cole Younger's thigh. It was Cole's first wound in what would turn out to be a long afternoon for him. Manning reloaded, looked up, and saw Bill Chadwell sitting on his horse a half-block away. Manning took deliberate aim and sent a bullet spiraling through Chadwell's heart.

Meanwhile, from his window on the third floor of the hotel, Wheeler was using his four cartridges to snipe at the invaders. He fired at Jim Younger, but the round went high. After reloading, he saw Clel Miller bent over his saddle trying to tighten a cinch. Wheeler rested his ancient Sharps on the window sill, aimed at the outlaw, and pulled the trigger. Clel Miller—already bleeding from the face—fell dead.

Up and down Division Street, the outlaws were being gunned down. Chadwell and Miller were dead, one of the outlaw's horses was down, and two more were running aimlessly along the road.

Horseless, Bob Younger took cover behind an outside stairwell near the bank. By then, several unarmed citizens had begun hurling rocks at him. "Stone him!" they shouted. "Stone him!" While little damage was done to the outlaw, the shouts added to the pandemonium.

Cole Younger saw that Miller was down and rode over to him. He jumped off his horse and turned his old guerrilla buddy over. At the same instant that he realized Miller was dead, a bullet smashed into Younger's hip. He retrieved both of Miller's revolvers and jumped back on his horse.

Manning, the man who had killed Chadwell, was coolly picking his targets and firing away. Bob Younger, crouching behind the same stairwell that Manning was firing from, decided to take the townsman out. He studied the arrangement of the stairwell for a moment, then positioned himself to shoot up through the stairs. As he aimed his revolver, a

146

bullet from the third floor of the hotel smashed his right elbow. Young Wheeler had found his mark again.

Then came a feat that was so incredible that it was mentioned by every citizen who later gave an interview about the raid.

The town physician, Dr. D. J. Whiting, who had been watching the combat through his window and saw Bob Younger get shot, tells it best: "The outlaw took his revolver in his left hand, jumped up in the air, turned clear around, and threw out his right foot as if kicking the stones [being] thrown by [residents] Hobbs and Streater." Bob snapped off a round at Manning, then fired one at storekeeper Bates. The ball went in Bates's cheek and came out his ear.

The chaos was growing even more desperate as other citizens found weapons. Jim Younger took a rifle ball in his shoulder.

The blood of outlaws and citizens alike soaked Northfield's once-peaceful streets.

Now the outlaws began trying to retreat. Cole Younger and Charlie Pitts attempted to load Clel Miller's body onto the back of Cole's horse. But the gunfire was so heavy that Cole finally mounted his horse and prepared to ride off.

Bob Younger abandoned his stairwell. He stepped out into the street and called to his brother Jim to catch a horse. Once mounted, he proceeded to pull the horseless Charlie Pitts up behind him. Then, with Jim Younger leading Bob's horse, the last group of outlaws took flight. With them, they took a mere twenty-six dollars and some pocket change.

When the citizens of Northfield rushed into the bank, they found Joseph Heywood lying facedown, with blood and brains oozing slowly from a hole in his temple. He was dead.

When his widow found out, she said of his actions, "I would not have wanted him to do otherwise."

The news quickly spread that another resident had been murdered by the outlaws. Nicholas Gustafson, a recent Swedish immigrant, had been in a carpenter's shop a block from the bank when the robbery began. The carpenter, John Olson, said he and Gustafson had been working down in the basement when they heard the gunfire. As they stepped outside to see what the shooting was about, an outlaw on a buckskin horse rode up and ordered them back inside. Olson complied immediately, but Gustafson didn't understand English. Jesse James repeated his order, then shot the unfortunate Swede between the eyes when he failed to comply.

The consensus among the citizens of Northfield was to let the corpses of Clel Miller and Bill Chadwell lie where they fell. This decision was partly meant to be a ghoulish rebuttal to any Northfield boys who thought they had seen anything dashing about the raiders.

In the due course of time, the dits and dots began to click across a thousand miles of Minnesota telegraph wire and a thousand Minnesotans answered the call to join the pursuit of the outlaws. Northfield residents were well-represented in the posse .

For the Youngers, the race to the Arkansas River would be their last. Each was critically wounded, and they were leaving blood trails for the manhunters to follow every painful mile they traveled.

Near Mankato, the James brothers elected to go on alone. They made it to the Arkansas River and eventually crossed into Missouri.

The posse finally caught up with the Youngers in a marshy slough on the edge of Lake Hanska. The pursuers quickly sealed off the exits, and another firefight ensued. Pinned down, the outlaws were sitting ducks for the well-armed possemen. Charlie Pitts was killed, and Cole, Bob, and Jim Younger were literally shot to pieces before Cole tied a bloody white handkerchief to a stick and signaled their surrender.

With life sentences handed out to the Youngers, and with Frank having been granted amnesty for his crimes, the saga of the James-Younger Gang had one just one chapter remaining. It would finally be written in St. Joseph, Missouri. On the third day of April, 1882, a wannabe desperado and newly recruited gang member named Bob Ford shot Jesse in the back as he was adjusting a picture on his wall. Ford expected to get a $5,000 reward for the murder. He never received a dime, however, and was himself murdered by a James sympathizer.

The inscription on Jesse's tombstone reflected the feelings of many Missourians when they heard the news of the outlaw's death:

JESSE W. JAMES
DIED APRIL 3, 1882
34 YEARS, 6 MONTHS, 28 DAYS OLD
Murdered by a coward whose name
Is not worthy to be printed here

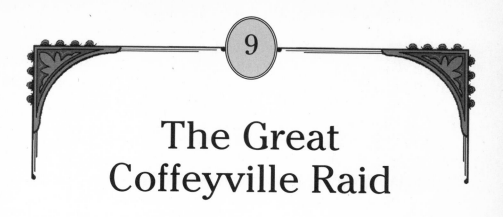

The Great Coffeyville Raid

At about four o'clock on the morning of October 5, 1892, five men broke camp on the Verdigras River in southeastern Kansas. They swung up onto their horses and headed for a small farming community four miles to the north. There they intended to ride into the history books by committing the most daring robbery of the century. This little band of horsemen planned to hold up two banks in the same town at the same time. No other gang in history—not even the incomparable James-Younger band—had been able to pull off such a feat.

When the smoke cleared, people in Kansas would date their calendars before and after that day for fifty years.

For three years the Dalton Gang had cast a shadow over the Great Plains.

Bob, Grat, and Emmett were born in Cass County, Missouri, a place that bred hard men who were clannish and wary of strangers.

Mother Adeline married Lewis Dalton when she was six-teen. She was an aunt to the notorious Younger brothers, but with a noteworthy twist. Adeline was a God-fearing woman who supported her husband in all of his extrava-gant, ill-judged endeavors. And she nurtured her children as well as she could in whatever homestead the family might find itself dwelling.

Early in their marriage, Lewis was the owner of a saloon. But he soon drank up his profits and went bankrupt. He switched to breeding slow racehorses and again ended up going broke. Eventually, Lewis abandoned his family to travel the medicine show circuit, hustling patent remedies which were said to contain twice as much alcohol as medic-inal ingredients—with a dash of opium in each bottle for good measure. Lewis Dalton was constantly on the road, but he must have made it home every year or so. Adeline bore him fifteen children.

After Cass County, the family moved to Montgomery County, Kansas, then to Locust Hill in Indian Territory and then to Kingfisher, northwest of Oklahoma City. It was there that the Dalton brothers began to gain a reputation as peo-ple to avoid.

Bob was six feet tall, mostly lean bone and gristle. In addition to being a ladies' man, he gained a reputation as the most accurate marksman in the territory. Grat was an inch taller and a bit fleshier. Already an alcoholic, he was unbeaten in his many fist-fights. One writer later said that he was "tough as a carbuncle—and about as touchy." Emmett, shorter than his brothers, had no special skills or addictions, and mostly just followed along.

One day in 1887, Bob and Grat headed east for Fort Smith, just across the border in Arkansas. When they crossed back into Indian Territory, they were duly commis-sioned United States deputy marshals, riding for Isaac Parker's federal district court. Parker, called the "hanging judge" for obvious reasons, served on the bench for twenty-one years. During his tenure, he sentenced 160 men to the gallows. His jurisdiction extended over 70,000 square miles of the most dangerous country on the continent. Before Parker's career ended, sixty-five of his deputies would be killed in the line of duty. When Bob and Grat Dalton pinned on their badges, fifteen deputies had been slain the preceding year.

The first thing the boys did when they returned to the Indian Nations was to sign Emmett up as a posseman.

For a while, the brothers did well. Old court records give evidence that they made some risky arrests, including one in which Grat took a bullet through the shoulder. During their brief tour as lawmen, the brothers engaged in several firefights in which they were badly outmanned. But Bob's Winchester Model 73 always prevailed.

The Daltons might have gone down in history as lawmen equal to such legends such Heck Thomas, Bill Tilghman, and Chris Madsen. But it wasn't to be. The brothers soon began to break the law more often than they enforced it. Eight months after assuming their duties, they were fully paid-up whiskey brokers, selling their bootleg jack throughout the Oklahoma and Indian Territories. After an investigation by United States Commissioner W. S. Fitzpatrick, Bob and Emmett were summarily fired. Two weeks later, Grat got his pink slip for brutally pistol-whipping a gambler he had arrested.

After their brief stint as lawmen, the brothers wasted little time finding other ways to make a living. They stole three separate herds of horses in the Indian Territory and spirited them to Baxter, Kansas, a notorious mecca for the criminal element. During their third trip, they barely escaped a posse. Legend and Emmett's autobiography say that they slipped out of a brothel in their socks, cashed a horse-buyer's check, gathered up two accomplices, and then fled to greener pastures.

They ended up in Santa Rosa, New Mexico, where they ran out of money and imprudently decided to hold up a faro game. This was their first armed robbery, and it showed. The brothers walked in with their guns drawn and found themselves facing some very angry silver miners. In the gunfight that followed, Emmett was shot in the elbow. The outlaws left empty-handed and headed to California at a dead run.

The brothers arrived at the farm of their brother Bill near Paso Robles in January 1891. For a few weeks, they worked at slopping hogs and tilling the soil. But they found farm labor in California about as hard, boring, and unfulfilling as it was back in Kingfisher.

On February 9, Bob, Emmett, Bill Mulhane, and Charley Bryant held up the Southern Pacific Railroad's Train No. 17 at a little water stop called Alila in Tulare County. The take was less than a thousand dollars. Grat was too drunk to ride, so he stayed home with brother Bill.

This robbery didn't go smoothly either. A shootout erupted, and the fireman of No. 17 was mortally wounded. The robbers soon fled California with a $1,500 bounty on each of their heads.

Back in Paso Robles, Grat sobered up quickly when a posse whisked him off to jail to stand trial for the bank robbery. Incredibly, he was found guilty even though a dozen witnesses testified that he'd been sleeping it off in Bill's barn when the robbery occurred. But Grat wasn't one to be inconvenienced for long. While awaiting sentencing in the rickety Tulare County Jail, he escaped and headed across half a continent to the Indian Territory. Eventually, he located his brothers hiding out in a wilderness area known as the Triangle Country.

While on a horse-stealing mission, Bob killed a pursuer and badly wounded another. This earned the brothers a writ for murder with Judge Isaac Parker's name on it.

By May 1891, the gang consisted of the Daltons, Mulhane, Bryant, and two newcomers, Bill Doolin and Bitter Creek George Newcomb.

Bob took up housekeeping with Flo Quick, described as a seductive beauty who began spending a lot of time snooping around telegraph offices.

The Daltons and Doolin held up a Santa Fe train at Wharton, Oklahoma. The take was small, and another railroad employee was killed.

Next up was the Kansas, Arkansas & Texas (locally referred to as the KATY) train at LaLaetta on September 15, 1891. Again, the take was small, about $2,500. With Deputy U.S. Marshall Heck Thomas on their trail, the gang members were becoming desperate for a more lucrative score.

They soon set their sights on a backwoods depot about forty miles south of Arkansas City, Kansas. It was called the Red Rock Station, and the gang intended to board and rob the train when it stopped there. Supposedly, Flo had seduced a telegraph operator, who reported that the train was carrying $70,000, part of an annual payment owed to local Indian tribes.

Unfortunately for the outlaws, it was also carrying a heavily armed group of lawmen led by Heck Thomas and his 8-gauge shotgun. Bob Dalton claimed later that he sensed the presence of the guards, so they let the train pass. The boys pounced on a second train which appeared about forty-five minutes later. Their prize was less than $3,000, so they testily yanked off a guard's gold watch and took his lunch box.

After the Red Rock debacle, the gang split up. A posse was close behind, so close that when they left, Flo abandoned her wardrobe, including some frilly Montgomery Ward negligees, as she fled.

The gang members reunited near Tulsa and planned their next robbery. They decided to hit another KATY train, this time in the town of Adair. The robbery started out smoothly but quickly degenerated. Unknown to the outlaws, this train carried eight guards donated to the railroad company by the Indian Police. A massive shootout ensued, and the gang galloped madly down Main Street. They were free and out of harm's way when, according to the local press, the riders fired about twenty rounds at two unarmed men who were watching the fireworks from the porch of a general store. Both men were hit.

And both men were respected townsmen.

One man died, and the other was severely wounded. Now the public's outrage was leveled against the Daltons. Emmett, in his self-serving autobiography, entitled *Beyond the Law*, called the dead man's wound "trifling" and blamed poor medical treatment for the man's death.

Practically everyone else saw it differently.

The KATY offered a reward of $5,000 for each participant in the robbery—dead or alive—collectively the largest bounty offered until that time for a band of outlaws. And fresh murder warrants were issued by Judge Parker.

From this point on, professional manhunters prepared to give chase to the Dalton boys.

Bob Dalton read the signs immediately: It was time to move on. Dakota, Montana, Washington state—anywhere except the the Oklahoma Territory, where the boys were no longer welcome.

One more job, Bob told his men—one big job. Then they could head for the Big Sky country. Time was of the essence, though.

Heck Thomas, with a small posse of expert trackers and a handful of warrants, had been on the trail of the gang from the first moment he heard about the pillaging at Adair. A gray-thatched and gray-mustachioed man who stood with a kind of military erectness, Thomas always gave his quarry a chance to surrender. But if the suspect didn't immediately throw up his hands, the lawman would start blasting with his 8-gauge shotgun. After he retired, it was estimated that Thomas had arrested 200 men in the line of duty and had killed twenty-four.

Riding with Bob Dalton toward the Kansas border were brothers Grat and Emmett, as well as Dick Broadwell and

Bill Power. Power was a Texan, short and burly, who had migrated to the territory to work as a cowhand. Broadwell, the son of a Kansas farmer, had punched cattle in Texas before he hooked up with the Daltons. Both men had ridden with the gang since its inception but only on an "as-needed" basis. (The hard, proven gunmen, Bill Doolin and Bitter Creek Newcomb, had quit the gang just after the raid on Adair. Later, Doolin would found his own gang and become a more successful leader than Bob Dalton. He lasted in the outlaw business until 1896, when he was gunned down by Heck Thomas.)

By the end of September, Bob was desperate. Thomas was only a day behind, following relentlessly. Because of the reward and the disgust felt toward the gang by most citizens, the desperadoes had nowhere to hole up.

Finally, the tired riders hid out for a week in some timbered area near the Mashed-O Ranch south of Tulsa. It was there that Bob revealed his plan.

He had decided to rob two banks in a place where he'd once lived. The town was Coffeyville, Kansas.

The outlaws arrived at the P. L. Davis farm on the evening of October 4 and made camp in the dense brush near Onion Creek. They were four miles west of Coffeyville.

For Grat Dalton, the party still rolled on. Emmett, in his autobiography, records that Grat drank vast quantities of whiskey while the others double-checked the deadly tools of their trade.

In 1892, the Winchester rifle, the Colt Army revolver, and the .44-40 round were the predominant choice of outlaws, lawmen, and civilians alike. The Model 86 Winchester saddle gun wasn't extremely powerful, but it was light and accurate up to 200 yards. The 1873 Colt Peacemaker, commonly known as the Colt Army, had a standard barrel length of $4^3/_4$ inches. It didn't fire as clean a blast as today's handguns. If you were on the receiving end, you might find flame and powder particles coming at you with the lead. The .44-40 brass cartridges were popular because they were inter-changeable—they fit both the rifle and the handgun.

The gang slept fitfully until 4 a.m., then moved out.

By the fall of 1892, Coffeyville was the kind of town many mainstream Americans would have liked to call home. In fact, 3,500 people did just that. It was not wide open and roaring like Dodge City, but it wasn't puritanical either.

The town prospered as a supply and market center for a rising number of homesteads and small ranches scattered throughout the county. On Walnut Street, for instance, J. T. Isham owned and operated a mercantile and hardware store beside R. Adamson and the Wells brothers, who packed and exported quail and prairie chickens to eastern markets. Across the street, J. J. Barndollar ran a grocery store next to the Southern Hotel, owned and operated by the Kloehr brothers. Adjacent to the hotel was the First National Bank of Coffeyville. The owner, Tom Ayers, had held a monopoly on the banking business until C. M. Condon founded a rival bank across the street in 1886.

The economic vigor of the community, though, came from what twentieth-century poets would call "amber waves of grain." Locally, it was known as Turkey Red.

Red was a hardy strain of wheat. Originally cultivated in Russia, Turkey Red was brought into Kansas by Mennonite settlers of German stock. Red thrived in the heat and didn't need a lot of water. And it was destined to make Kansas the wheat capital of the world.

So, by the last decade of the nineteenth century, Coffeyville was a thriving little community with a burgeoning cash crop and a nonexistent crime rate. In the 1870s, Coffeyville had been an upstart cattle town with the crime and violence associated with boomtowns. But the town fathers had never resorted to hiring a "town-tamer"—

a professional gunfighter like Bill Hickock, Bat Masterson, or the Earp brothers. And there was a reason for this.

Around Coffeyville, the defenders of law and order were ordinary men who chose to band together and regulate their own town in their own manner. Normally peaceable men, they had also learned the most important rule a gentleman ever learns—which is precisely when to stop being one. The Bender family paid the ultimate price to find this out.

In the 1870s, the Benders had lived near a well-traveled road on the outskirts of Coffeyville. Their modest farm-house doubled as an inn. But family members eventually got the idea of robbing the travelers who stayed overnight at their lodgings. Prospects should be well-heeled and traveling solo, and they couldn't have connections to south-eastern Kansas.

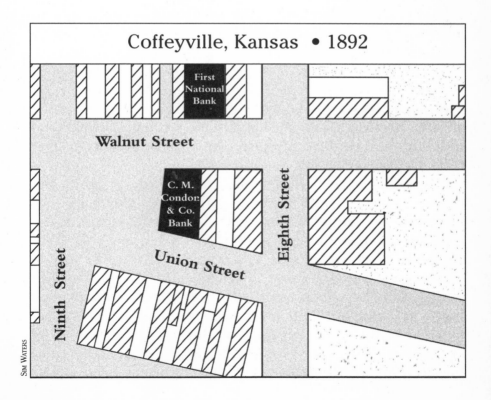

Coffeyville, Kansas • 1892

Almost overnight, the Benders began to prosper, and certain lodgers who checked in for a night seemed to disappear off the face of the earth.

Legend and old newspaper clippings reveal that the family would attend to select guests in an assembly-line manner. Ma would feed him, Pa would crush the back of his skull with a hatchet, and brother would slide him down a trapdoor to the cellar, where daughter Kate would cut the unfortunate victim's throat with a boning knife.

In due course, some of Coffeyville's leading citizens got wind of the Benders' enterprise and held a private meeting. Later that night, the Benders simply disappeared off the face of the earth.

"That Arkansas quicksand's bottomless," one citizen was heard to say. "We just ran the whole dadgummed thing in—horses, wagon, and Benders."

No organized law and order here. Just spot a problem and solve it.

The five outlaws arrived in Coffeyville the next morning shortly after nine o'clock. The streets were filled with people, but they paid no attention to the five strangers who rode in quiet as smoke.

Having lived near Coffeyville for a couple of years, the Daltons tried to avoid being recognized by gluing tufts of horsehair to their faces. The effect was ridiculous. Even the most casual observer would also have noted that the riders were all armed to the teeth in a town of unarmed people.

They rode their horses up Walnut Street and reined in between the two banks. But the hitching post they remembered as being only a hair's-breath from the First National had been temporarily dug up so that the street could be graded. They hesitated for a moment, then galloped their horses into an alley across from the downtown plaza where the banks were sitting. There they dismounted and hitched their mounts in the back of a lot owned by Police Judge D. Munn. A minute later, an oil tanker pulled by two horses showed up. The teamster secured the horses to the same hitching post.

The outlaws marched back up the plaza in two rows. The three in front, Grat, Power, and Broadwell, peeled off at Walnut and went into the C. M. Condon & Company Bank. A few seconds later Bob and Emmett crossed the plaza and entered the First National.

Unknown to the bank robbers, a long-time resident of the town saw the trio go into the Condon bank. He thought he recognized Grat Dalton, and peered in the bank window to make sure. Seeing Grat point a Winchester at the cashier, the citizen turned and tore through the streets shouting an alarm.

The citizens of Coffeyville soon converged at the two hardware stores. The owners and clerks hastily handed out rifles, shotguns, and ammunition. Now armed, the men positioned themselves about the plaza and took cover.

Inside the Condon bank were the owner, the bookkeeper, and the cashier, Charles M. Ball. The outlaws ordered Ball to open the vault. The cashier told Grat that there was a time lock on the vault and that it couldn't be opened for another ten minutes. Grat had to make a decision. He figured Ball was lying, so he threatened to kill all the employees. But in the end, he decided to wait it out. Eight minutes later, a citizen from behind a barricade shot through the bank window.

The battle was on.

It was smoother sailing at the First National Bank. Bob and Emmett had no trouble seizing the employees and taking control of the lobby. Bob forced the cashier to gather up all the money in the vault and stuff it into a gunny sack. Emmett grabbed the money, and Bob rounded up all the bank employees, forcing them toward the front door. Then the guns started blazing. Bob abandoned the hostages and sprinted toward the rear door. Emmett wasn't far behind.

Charles T. Gump was one of the first citizens to rush into the Isham Brothers Hardware Store. He ignored the proffered rifle, arming himself with a handgun instead. He stepped out onto the street at the same instant Bob Dalton came through the rear door of the bank into the alley. Gump snapped off a shot and missed. Bob Dalton then drilled him. Gump was the first casualty of the fight. He was pulled back into the hardware store by his friends.

Lucius M. Baldwin, a clerk at the Read Bros. General Merchandise, was next to fall. He too had armed himself at Isham's. As he walked toward Bob and Emmett, Bob Dalton ordered him to stop. Baldwin ignored him and kept walking forward. Bob raised his carbine, aimed, and put a slug through Baldwin's chest. The clerk staggered backward, dropped to his knees, and collapsed. He died three hours later.

The civilians had started firing at irregular intervals and from various positions. George Clubine stationed himself in front of Rummel Bros. Drug Store with a carbine. Bob Dalton raised his rifle again, and instantly fired. Clubine's body jerked violently with the impact of the bullet and he died as he fell. Charles Brown scooped up Clubine's weapon and aimed at the outlaws. He, too, was quickly gunned down.

Thomas Ayers, the cashier at the First National Bank, had left the building when Bob and Emmett ran out the back door. He raced to Isham's, seized a Winchester, and joined the battle. Bob Dalton shot him in the face. T. Arthur Reynolds, a customer at Isham's when the shooting started, joined the fray and was shot in the foot.

By now, the gunfire was a continuous roar. Smoke clouded the streets like fog.

Even though the townspeople were dying, the momentum had begun to change.

The Dalton Gang had made at least two mistakes. The

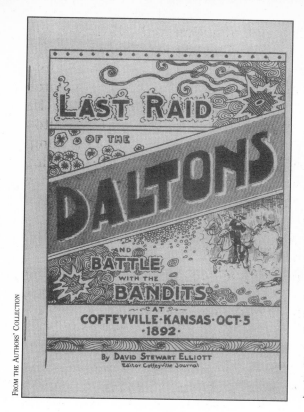

Last Raid of the Daltons and Battle with the Bandits *was published by* Coffeyville Journal *Editor David Stewart Elliott and quickly became a collector's item. Elliott saw the gun battle and immediately went to his office to write an account of it. This reproduction of the 1892 booklet is from the Coffeyville Historical Society's Dalton Defenders Museum.*

first had been to stash their horses too far away. The second was not to leave someone to hold them so that they could be brought to the outlaws if they got into trouble.

Meanwhile, inside the Condon bank, the outlaws were coming under heavy fire from the guns around Isham's. Grat, Broadwell, and Power conferred briefly, then ran into the street. Under a hail of gunfire, they headed toward the alley where the horses were tied. Grat was wounded as he approached the hitching post. He dove behind the oil tanker and began cranking off wild rounds. Bill Power, the mysterious Texan, fell dead beside his already dead horse.

Two citizens, John Kloehr and Marshall Connelly, were inching their way toward the hitching post where the bandits'

Surviving mem-bers of the Dalton Gang were held in the Coffeyville Jail until their trials.

horses were tethered. Grat stood up and shot Connelly through the throat. Dick Broadwell used the occasion to swing up on his horse and ride off. Kloehr, conceded by many to be the best marksman in southeastern Kansas, shot Broadwell through the back at 200 yards. Broadwell kept riding but died in the saddle about a mile out of town.

Bob and Emmett Dalton shot their way up Eighth Street and finally made it into the alley near where the horses were hitched. Bob was hit by a round fired from the hardware store but managed to keep firing until he was shot through the chest by Kloehr.

Several of the outlaws' horses had been hit, and were wallowing on the ground, snorting in pain and fear. Grat found his mount still tied to the rail and tried to climb aboard. Kloehr killed him, too.

Emmett, who was carrying the money bag, had some-how reached the alley unscathed. He jumped up on his horse and rode west for about a hundred yards. Then, in one of the most courageous deeds ever perpetrated by a western outlaw, he turned and rode back into the gunfire to try to pick up his brother Bob. As he reached down for Bob's hand, businessman Carey Seamen shot him in the back with both barrels of a 12-gauge shotgun. Emmett dropped into the alley beside his brothers and waved his uninjured hand in a feeble gesture of surrender.

Finally, after fifteen minutes of unrelenting gunfire, the town was quiet. Outlaws and citizens lay side by side.

It was then that the surviving citizens of Coffeyville rushed to the scene and showed their true colors.

Instead of putting a bullet between Emmett's eyes on behalf of their fallen comrades, the townspeople whisked him over to a doctor's office.

By the next day, Heck Thomas and a group of lawmen had converged on Coffeyville. Citizens reconstructed the battle, and it later went down in history as the second-greatest accomplishment of townspeople defending their town. (Most scholars agree that the residents' defense of Northfield, Minnesota, against the James Gang ranks as number one, based on the caliber of opposition the towns-people faced.)

What went wrong with the raid on Coffeyville? A combination of haste, poor planning, and a determined group of citizens foiled the robbers.

Heck Thomas and his posse had been hunting the Daltons for several months. At the time of Coffeyville, they were only a day behind the outlaws. The Daltons wanted to make a big strike so they could "disappear." In their haste, they did no reconnaissance, relying only on faulty memories. The hitching rail had been moved, so they had to tether their horses nearly 300 yards from the banks. This gave the outlaws no margin of error.

Finally, the townspeople wasted no time retrieving guns and ammunition and proved to be too much for the out-manned and outgunned Daltons.

For Emmett Dalton, it was touch and go for a few days. A doctor bandaged his wounds, and he was not expected to live. But the tough outlaw surprised everyone and eventually recovered from his wounds.

Emmett was tried and convicted for armed robbery and sentenced to thirty years in the Kansas State Prison. While there, he wrote a popular book about the Dalton Gang, entitled *When the Daltons Rode*. He was pardoned in 1907 by Kansas Governor E. W. Hoch. Emmett married and settled in Tulsa, where he became a police officer.

On July 13, 1937, Emmett Dalton died peacefully in Hollywood, California.

High Mountain Robbery

*In less than three minutes, every avenue
of escape was closed, and a dozen or more good
marksmen awaited the robbers' escape.*
— Claude Wakefield, *One Boy's Life*, 1960

The Browns Park area in northwest Colorado lies on a plateau in the Rocky Mountains. About a hundred miles southeast is a wide-open space called the White River Valley. Near the middle of valley lies the town of Meeker.

At the turn of the nineteenth century, Browns Park was sparsely populated. Cabins hewn from slash pines dotted the landscape. Trout streams were numerous, and elk and mule deer plentiful. The plant life was dense, with huge trees that had been undisturbed for centuries. Aspens, especially, were so abundant that a nearby town chose to name itself after them.

The few paths leading into the park were narrow and slippery. Visitors had to ascend these trails single-file, gingerly picking their way through wet rock and gravel. But if these visitors were outdoorsmen seeking to get back to nature for a week or two while living off the land, they'd never make it to the top. Others were already ensconced there, and these residents weren't looking to make new friends.

Browns Park was one of the permanent hideouts of Butch Cassidy and his Hole in the Wall Gang.

Indisputably the most successful of the nineteenth-century outlaw leaders, Cassidy shared his time on the run among his Robbers' Roost hideout in Idaho, the Hole in the Wall near Jackson Hole, Wyoming, and Browns Park. Browns Park is where he and his gang happened to be in the fall of 1896.

The gang was hiding out because they were hot. In late September 1896, Cassidy and his hand-picked cohorts had looted the bank of Montpelier, Colorado of $75,000. As in most of the robberies Cassidy planned and led, nobody got hurt. So no fiery-eyed posse of cowboys and Idaho lawmen would be hounding the gang.

But the Pinkertons would.

Hired by western bankers associations to pursue Cassidy and his followers to the ends of the earth, if necessary, these tenacious agents and operatives would soon be poking throughout Idaho and Wyoming looking for the perpetrators. Cassidy, who saw these professional manhunters more as nuisances than threats, decided to spend the winter laying low in Browns Park.

Already there was an assembly of misfits—petty thieves, crooked gamblers, outlaw wannabes. The only criterion for access to any of Cassidy's safe havens was that the candidate had to be wanted by some law enforcement agency, or think he was. That, and an eagerness to take other peoples' money.

These hangers-on could stay as long as they wanted, but their chances of riding with Cassidy and his men were nil. Butch Cassidy only raided with proven freebooters he'd known for years.

Among the fifteen or so loiterers at the Browns Park campsite when the gang returned from Montpelier were three small-time hoods who yearned to play at the big casino. Jim Shirley, "Kid" Pierce, and George Law (later identified as George Bain) were rustlers and horse thieves who had worn out their welcome in polite society.

When the Wild Bunch (as the Hole in the Wall Gang was also called) returned from Idaho with saddlebags bulging with greenbacks and gold coins, Shirley, Pierce, and Law listened with a mixture of awe and envy as Cassidy and the Sundance Kid described in detail how the robbery had gone down. They decided it was time to strike out on their own.

Jim Shirley, about forty-five, was thought to have emerged as the leader of the group. Before showing up in Browns Park, Shirley had plied his trade up in Montana and Wyoming. His trade was small-time cattle rustling. In the spring of 1896, he'd found himself "posted" by the Wyoming Cattle Buyers Association. This meant, in Shirley's case, that if he ran across any of the association's numerous assassins, that particular gunfighter would be paid a $500 bounty if he killed Shirley. The rustler prudently relocated to Colorado.

Not much is known about Pierce except that he was young by outlaw standards. Said to be about twenty-one, he seldom spoke to anyone in Browns Park except Shirley and Law.

George Law was a ne'er-do-well cowboy who'd ridden the ranges of Colorado for years, always driving cows for somebody else. About thirty-five years old, he'd procured horses for the Wild Bunch before some of their raids, and was always welcome in any of the Cassidy camps.

There wasn't much collective bank-robbing experience to draw from among the three collaborators. But there were plenty of Hole in the Wallers at the Browns Park camp eager to give advice. Shirley reportedly discussed the plan with Cassidy, who gave him a few pointers and wished him luck.

Shirley, Law, and Kid Pierce then packed their horses with provisions, cleaned their weapons, and rode off into the night.

Below Browns Park, on the White River plateau, towns and hamlets had begun to dot the land. Without ever having been there, the conspirators decided to rob the Bank of Meeker, Colorado.

Meeker was founded in 1868 by Major John Wesley Powell. In its early days, the town served as winter quarters for U.S. Army officers. Later, the buildings were turned over to the Department of Indian Affairs, and an Indian agency was established.

An agent was appointed, a gentle Quaker whose only mission, as he saw it, was to serve his clients. His foremost clients were bloodthirsty Utes who gleefully responded to his kindnesses with arrogance, insult, and disorderly mischief. As long as the idealistic Quakers were in charge, the Utes were able to take advantage of their mentors. One of the ways the Indians made money was gambling on horse races they staged. The Utes even

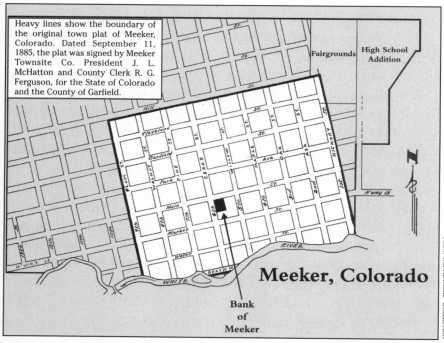

Heavy lines show the boundary of the original town plat of Meeker, Colorado. Dated September 11, 1885, the plat was signed by Meeker Townsite Co. President J. L. McHatton and County Clerk R. G. Ferguson, for the State of Colorado and the County of Garfield.

Meeker, Colorado

Bank of Meeker

built a superb racetrack where they pitted their pintos against the horses of nearby ranchers. The stakes were high, and the Indians usually won.

But in 1878 a new Indian agent arrived, a fiery Protestant as different from his predecessor as day is from night. Nathan Meeker arrived with his wife and young daughter. They were also idealistic, but their sole aim in life was to convert the Utes from primitive savages to hard-working, God-fearing farmers.

Meeker commenced his campaign by plowing up the Indians' racetrack. The dust from the agent's plow had no sooner settled that the outraged Utes promptly responded by killing and scalping Meeker along with his ten male employees. The women and children were captured and the agency was burned.

After twenty-three days of captivity, the women were released, mainly through the intercession of a Ute woman named Chipeta. The Utes were then rounded up by the U.S. Army and moved to reservations in Utah and southwest Colorado.

In 1883, the Army sold all the buildings in the settlement to private buyers with the provision that they build a town and name it after the slain Indian agent. Since Meeker was a fanatic who regularly offended white visitors to the agency as well as the Utes, it is doubtful that the town would have been named for him without the Army's insistence.

In 1885, the town of Meeker was incorporated, and that same year a printing press was shipped in from nearby Leadville. Shortly thereafter, the *Meeker Herald*—a weekly newspaper still in circulation—cranked out its first edition.

A town marshall was duly elected, stores and businesses were built, and settlers arrived. In the fall of each year, Texas cattlemen would drive their herds through Meeker—this added excitement to the residents and extra money for the store owners. Life there revolved around simple pleasures, and the residents basked in their small-town security.

In 1893, a bank opened its doors for business. Named the Bank of Meeker, it occupied a part of the space in a hardware store on Main Street called the Hugus Building. By 1897, it would occupy a spot at the top of Meeker's civic landmarks.

At about 3 p.m. on October 13, 1896, George Law and Kid Pierce entered the front door of the Hugus Building. Simultaneously, Jim Shirley came in through the side door. Law walked past the counter of the hardware store and up to the cashier's window. There he pulled a revolver from his belt and ordered David Smith, the cashier, to raise his hands. When Smith hesitated, Law cranked off a shot near his head. The explosion deafened Smith and startled the employees of the hardware store.

"Get your hands up!" Law repeated.

Before Smith could respond, Law fired a second round. This time the psychological impact was instantaneous.

Smith threw his hands up and kept them there.

The two gunshots also got the attention of the bank manager and the other clerks. When they looked up from their ledgers, they found they were covered by a pistol held by Jim Shirley. One of the clerks later recalled for a Denver daily newspaper that the barrel of the revolver looked "big enough to sleep in."

On a peaceful afternoon in a peaceful town, two gunshots fired inside a bank attracted considerable attention. An unidentified citizen came out of the nearby Meeker Hotel, peered into the bank, and saw people with their hands raised. He raced to tell the sheriff while another man ran in the opposite direction shouting the alarm.

According to an article in the *Meeker Herald*, even the town drunk got in on the act. A rather snobbish lady flounced up the street and was about to enter the bank. The drunk, who was in front of the bank taking in the robbery, announced, "Don't go in there, lady! There's a robbery in progress." The woman, who apparently thought the drunk was much too free in dispensing his advice, replied, "I guess I know my business, and I'll go where I please!"

"Go on in, lady," the drunk replied. "Get your butt shot off." The *Herald* failed to reveal whether she continued into the bank.

Back in the bank, Law scooped $1,500 form the cash drawer into a sugar sack while Pierce covered the employees and customers. Shirley, walking by a gun rack in the rear of the store, noticed a gun rack with several weapons. He sauntered over, picked out three rifles which suited him, then went to the ammunition case and took out three boxes of ammo. Then he proceeded to leisurely load each weapon. Eyewitnesses later estimated that the outlaw took nearly ten minutes choosing and loading the firearms. While Shirley deliberated over the guns, George Law hurriedly counted the money in the sugar sack. Kid Pierce kept the captives covered in the bank lobby.

By the time the robbers decided to leave, the front door was being guarded by more than a dozen riflemen, including Town Marshal Ben Nichols. But the robbers came out the side door instead, using six citizens as shields. The procession marched to a corral behind the store where a freight wagon sat.

There Shirley spotted W. H. Clark about fifteen yards away. He wheeled and shot the citizen through the chest with his rifle. Clark fell in the dirt, kicking and moaning.

Shirley and Law began to untie horses from the wagon while Pierce guarded the hostages with a rifle.

The armed citizens, afraid of hitting their own friends and neighbors, withheld fire. Using buildings, wagons, and even horses for cover, they edged closer to the robbers, waiting for their chance.

Their break came when one of the captives broke free. As he ran down the street, the others scattered. Pierce opened fire at the fleeing hostages with his Winchester. Three men went down.

V. A. Dykeman, one of the hostages, told the editor of the *Meeker Herald* what happened next:

> There was a corral in back of the bank where they kept freight horses. Mr. H. S. Harp and F. N. J. Hantgen were behind the board fence. The outlaws had their horses tied to a freight wagon and soon as they [the hostages] broke out of line, Simp Harp and Frank J. Hantgen shot Shirley and the Kid. When Law saw them drop, he started to run down the street and somebody shot him in the back. I think it was Ben Nichols that got him. This old Shirley got shot through the back and through the heart. . . . As he fell, he dropped his rifle and pulled his revolver, and emptied it as he lay there on the street.

When Law saw his comrades fall, he turned and ran toward the White River. He was turning the corner around a building when two bullets felled him. He hung on for nearly an hour before he died. Pierce and Shirley were dead before they hit the ground. They were buried in the Highland Cemetery.

Coincidently, both of the town's doctors were out of town on hunting trips. Dr. French was hunting elk in Thornburg, and Dr. Young was in Coyote Basin. Link Talbert raced to Dr. French and brought him back to treat the wounded Meeker heroes. Each of them recovered nicely.

A Coroner's Jury found that the killings of the outlaws was justifiable homicide. The outlaws' bodies were turned over to an undertaker named Niblack, who prepared them for burial. The whole town convened at the Highland Cemetery outside Meeker. Law, Shirley, and Pierce were buried beneath wooden crosses in the Potter's Field section of the graveyard.

The town drunk had the final word. According to the *Meeker Herald*, Mrs. Ed Fairchild was among the crowd waiting to see the outlaws laid to rest. She pushed her way toward the pine boxes, but when she got close enough to see the bodies, she immediately fainted. No one seemed to know what to do until the drunk—later identified as Old Phil Barhart—spoke up. "Loosen her corset," he shouted. "Then she can breathe better."

11

The Planned Bank Robbery Watch

Fred Hammer is dead with a bullet in his brain, Luther Smalley and Adam [Richetti] are suffering from bullet wounds, and are in the hospital, after failing in an attempted holdup of the Mill Creek Bank Wednesday afternoon.
— Sulphur Times-Democrat

At 2:30 on the afternoon of March 9, 1932, a dozen men shuffled miserably in the cold of another late-winter Oklahoma day. The bank robbery watch was nothing like they'd imagined. Some retreated into the warm stores surrounding the First National Bank in Mill Creek. Others, dressed in heavy overcoats, stood outside, smoking an occasional cigarette to keep warm. They were farmers, clerks, lawyers, businessmen. The one thing they had in common was that they were all armed.

The bank robbery watches were the brainchild of the Oklahoma Bankers Association. Hundreds of banks in the state had been robbed during the last few years—so many that the Association had resorted to placing bounties on the heads of robbers. This year alone, twelve banks had fallen to the holdup men. Law enforcement seemed powerless to stop the heavily armed gangs. Desperate, the Association came up with a new strategy. Armed "vigilante" groups were formed and trained to lie in wait in strategic positions outside banks, hoping to get a shot at any bandit who might ride into the armed camp. These watches were manned by volunteers from the community—the "home guard," as local newspapers called them. As an incentive, the Association promised to pay the group $500 for each robber who was killed. Any robber captured alive would bring $100. The money was to be split among those involved in the capture or killing of a bandit. Nineteen thirty-two was one of the bleakest years of the Great Depression, and a bounty of any amount would make a notable addition to a strained budget. Best of all, members of the home guard were to remain anonymous so that other gangsters couldn't retaliate.

The First National Bank of Mill Creek had twice been the target of robberies. On July 11, 1927, two men held it up for more than $4,000. One bandit was captured and sentenced to fifteen years in prison. Four years later, three outlaws made a daring getaway after robbing the bank of a small amount of cash. These bandits were also apprehended.

But on that cold afternoon in 1932, those robberies seemed to have happened centuries ago. The men manning the stakeout had lost interest, and just wanted to go home.

Adam "Eddie" Richetti was born August 5, 1909, in Strawn, Texas. He didn't know it then, of course, but his execution some thirty years later would mark an end to the "gangsterism" that had beset America in the Prohibition era.

Eddie was the eighth of nine children born to Bartolomeo and Elisabetta Richetti. The family moved to Lehigh, Oklahoma, where Bartolomeo put his children to work on local farms and in area mines. As a sideline, he sold bootleg beer to the miners.

Eddie got into trouble early. On one occasion, he stole typewriters and a baseball glove from a local school. With a friend named Otis Harper, Richetti committed several burglaries. When local law enforcement officials became suspicious of their activities, the two packed up and moved to Hammond, Indiana.

It was there that they committed one of the strangest robberies ever recorded in Hammond. In the summer of 1928, August Geber, a middle-aged businessman, was out with two friends when his car broke down. He was attempting to get it started when another car pulled up. Eddie Richetti and Otis Harper jumped out and robbed Geber at gunpoint, taking all the money he had, which was a twenty-dollar bill. His two companions, a Mrs. Rominger and Mrs. Newhall, were then forced to give the robbers their gold wedding rings.

After robbing the trio, the bandits volunteered to help Geber get his car started. Then they ordered him to drive them around while they sweet-talked the women they'd robbed. Mrs. Rominger, playing along with the bandits, suggested that she call a young female friend to join their "party." Richetti and Harper agreed, and ordered Geber to drive Mrs. Rominger to her home so she could use the telephone. But as soon as she stepped out of the car, the frightened woman ran to a policeman who happened to be in the area and reported the robbery. Richetti and Harper were arrested and pled guilty to armed robbery. Sentenced to one to ten years in prison, they were incarcerated at the Indiana State Reformatory in Pendleton.

Many of the townspeople back in Lehigh couldn't believe that one of their own was a criminal. Elisabetta Richetti played on their hometown pride and coordinated a letter-writing campaign to get her son paroled. At least thirty letters of support were received by the warden, including two from the local sheriff and judge.

In October, 1930, Richetti received his parole and a one-way ticket back to Oklahoma.

179

He moved in with his sister and her husband, Luther "Blackie" Smalley. Within a short time, his parole officer reported that Richetti was unemployed and was suspected of at least one burglary.

In prison, Richetti had heard wild tales of fantastic wealth accumulated by bank robbers. In fact, John Dillinger had been incarcerated at Pendleton shortly before Richetti arrived. The convict grapevine was replete with tales of Dillinger's exploits. Inmates at Pendleton looked on the outlaw as if he were some god who could drop good luck upon his followers.

Richetti, who was a small sunken-faced man, was bent on forming a gang of bank robbers. His brother-in-law joined up, then helped Richetti recruit a former Seminole County deputy sheriff named Fred Hammer.

The three traveled all over Oklahoma casing banks. "Even small banks hold big money," Richetti told his starstruck followers. Maybe that's why they settled on the First National Bank of Mill Creek. Or maybe the small-town bank just looked easy.

At 2:30 p.m. on March 9, cashier Charlie Penner stood behind the teller's cage. Two bookkeepers, Vivian Dye and Paul Sparks, were also on duty. No customers were in the bank.

A 1932 Chevrolet Coupe pulled up and parked across the street directly in front of the bank. Two men got out. A third man sat in the car with the motor running.

The bored members of the bank robbery watch saw nothing suspicious. Across the street from the bank, at Young's Garage, grease monkeys toiled while members of the watch sat around a fire trying to keep warm. To pass the time, they swapped a day-old newspaper which contained yet another account of the kidnapping of Charles Lindbergh's baby.

Across the street, at the First National, two men stormed into the lobby. As soon as they entered, Fred Hammer—dressed in a pinstripe suit and coveralls—and Blackie Smalley—wearing a black suit—pulled pistols from their coats and ordered the three employees to lie on the floor.

But a suspicious Charlie Penner had time to trigger an alarm that had recently been installed.

Bells sounded in several businesses around the bank.

At Young's Garage, the surprised members of the home guard sprang into action. Using cars parked along the road for cover, they readied their guns and waited. According to a local newspaper account, the "vigilantes," as they were called, were armed with "Winchester [hunting] rifles and shotguns loaded with buckshot."

Inside the bank, Hammer moved behind the teller's cage

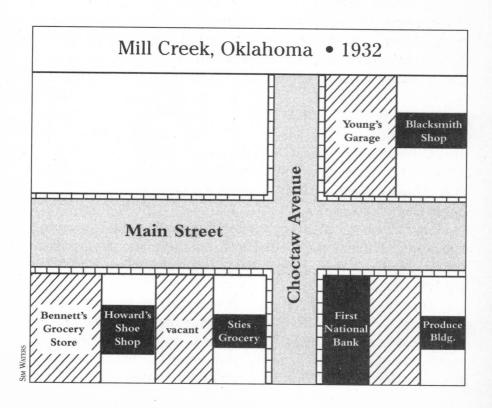

Mill Creek, Oklahoma • 1932

Young's Garage   Blacksmith Shop

Main Street

Choctaw Avenue

Bennett's Grocery Store   Howard's Shoe Shop   vacant   Sties Grocery   First National Bank   Produce Bldg.

Sim Waters

and scooped cash into a black leather handbag. He and Smalley were unaware that armed citizens were gathering at strategic points outside the bank.

Even Richetti, the supposed lookout, was oblivious to the danger.

Behind the teller's cage, near the rear of the bank, a vault stood with its door half-open. After Hammer finished taking the cash, he ordered Penner and Dye to get up. Penner rightly suspected that they were to be used as human shields. Knowing that a dozen trigger-happy vigilantes were lurking outside, he was determined to keep himself and his co-worker inside the bank. He grabbed Vivian Dye by the arm and shoved her into the vault. Then he dove inside. As Penner pulled the door shut, Hammer cursed and fired a round at him. The bullet hit the door, then ricocheted harmlessly into the floor.

Outside, the gunshot got the attention of the members of the bank robber watch. Had the gunmen killed one of the bank's employees? They strained to see. They knew that experienced bank robbers would bring hostages with them when they came out. The members didn't want to shoot their own friends and neighbors. The key to a successful defense of their town would be to wait until they had clear shots, then fire.

Inside the bank, Hammer and Smalley panicked. They could have picked up Paul Sparks, who was still lying on the floor. But they didn't.

Instead, they ran straight for the door, Hammer carrying the satchel filled with money. Bank officials would later count $830, somewhat less than the many thousands the robbers expected.

As they ran out, a fusillade erupted. Hammer was hit in the head. According to contemporary accounts, he fell on the steps leading out of the bank. A slug had pierced the right side of the head near the temple, then exited between the eyes. He was lifeless when he hit the sidewalk.

Blackie Smalley made it a few steps further. A shotgun blast riddled his body, then a rifle ball above the left eye dropped him. The bag of money lay between the robbers.

The gunplay caught Richetti completely off guard. One minute he was sitting in a brand-new getaway car dreaming of wealth, and the next he saw his "gang" cut to shreds by a group of local armed citizens. This was something he'd never factored into his plans.

Richetti saw a group of townspeople firing from cover in front of Young's Garage. He slammed the car into gear and screeched away, driving south. But after driving about seventy-five yards, he changed his mind. The getaway driver began backing down the street, firing a pistol at the townspeople. After cranking off a few rounds, he again drove away.

Blackie Smalley was wounded severely, but he wasn't dead. As the home guards turned their full attention to the getaway car, Smalley crawled down the sidewalk to where he'd dropped his gun. He picked up the pistol and raised it to a position where he could fire. Suddenly, a gun barrel was placed against his head.

"Drop it, or you're a dead man," someone said.

Smalley dropped the weapon, never knowing that his captor could have made more money by killing him.

With both his accomplices out of commission, Richetti was an enemy target. Hundreds of rounds were fired at the car. All the windows were blasted out, the front bumper was dragging the ground, and one of the casings was blown off. With dozens of bullet holes in it, the car smoked away.

Richetti was hit three times. He was wounded in the left arm, had a flesh wound to his left leg, and a deep wound to back of his neck. He drove south, his head swimming, and the car going slower and slower.

When he reached the P. W. South farm, the car quit. Richetti got out, climbed through a fence, then headed toward the South's barn. He staggered inside, trailing blood.

Realizing that the barn was the first place the cops would look, he decided to make for a stand of timber on a nearby hill. He crossed a creek, then fled into a wooded area. Exhausted, he sat down and waited for his pursuers to arrive.

Meanwhile, Deputy Sheriff Robert Donaldson and Under-Sheriff Pat Trotter raced from nearby Sulphur to Mill Creek. They hastily swore in a posse, then followed the trail of glass and twisted metal along the road.

At the South farm, they came upon the dead Chevrolet. The bandit's trail was easy to follow. Patches of blood led the posse to the wooded area where Richetti sat.

The posse fanned out, surrounding the grove. Someone yelled, "Reach skyward!"

The wounded man complied.

He was handcuffed and searched. The lawmen didn't find a weapon on him, but they did locate eleven .45-caliber bullets in his pocket.

Officers then ordered the wounded man to walk down to the police car.

After securing Richetti in the back of a car, they searched the Chevrolet. According to the March 10, 1932, issue of the *Johnston County Capital Democrat*, "the officers found a 12-gauge shotgun and a .30-30 rifle, both well-oiled."

The wounded robbers were taken to Sulphur Sanitarium for treatment. After two weeks, they were pronounced well enough to be transported to the nearby Tishomingo Jail.

On April, 5, 1932, Richetti and Smalley were tried and convicted of armed robbery. Both men were sentenced to one to ten years. They were then taken to McAllister State Penitentiary to serve their time. In a strange twist, Richetti and Smalley were released on bond less than four months later. Smalley, evidently a slow learner, was later killed by armed citizens when he attempted to rob a bank in Comanche, Oklahoma.

Richetti headed straight for the Cookson Hills. He'd once met Charles "Pretty Boy" Floyd when they were both working the oil fields in Earlsboro. Since the outlaw's "lieutenant" George Birdwell had been killed, Richetti knew that Floyd had a job opening.

Richetti met Floyd, possibly at Blackie Smalley's farm, and became a trusted friend and partner of the outlaw. In 1932 and 1933, they were involved in several robberies, shootings, and even the kidnappings of two different lawmen.

But, as the gangster era was coming to a close, the history books would record Adam Richetti as the only man ever convicted of the infamous Kansas City Massacre.

Frank "Jelly" Nash was a murderer, bank robber, kidnapper, and thief. He'd served time in several prisons, the latest being Leavenworth. He was tall, thin, and bald, with dark murderous eyes. After escaping from Leavenworth, Nash fled to Chicago and hooked up with another brutal murderer, Verne Miller. Miller had been a true World War I hero and law officer before joining forces with the mob, where he became a torpedo (thug), bank robber, and hit man.

By 1932, the Federal Bureau of Investigation under the leadership of J. Edgar Hoover had become the largest national police force in America. The rise of the bureau coincided with the rise of the Prohibition-era gangsters. The FBI had obtained legendary status for its killing of the notorious John Dillinger. One by one it was eliminating the most heinous gangsters. (Hoover had seen so many fugitives released or allowed to escape from prisons and jails across the country that it is thought that he issued an unwritten order for agents to shoot to kill.)

On June 16, 1933, the FBI arrested Jelly Nash at a resort in Hot Springs, Arkansas. Since the politicians and police forces of many American cities, including Hot Springs and Kansas City, were thoroughly corrupt, agents planned to take a furtive route by motorcar to Leavenworth.

Unfortunately, they had to pass through Kansas City. Along the way, they enlisted the aid of local law enforcement agencies. Inevitably, the route that agents had tried to keep secret leaked out. Frances Nash, the outlaw's wife, was notified by members of the underworld, and she contacted members of the Chicago mob.

After a series of roundabout negotiations, it was decided to try to free Nash before he got to Leavenworth.

Kansas City would be the perfect location.

It just so happened that Pretty Boy Floyd and Eddie Richetti had come into town the night before. As was the custom of criminals, they had contacted Johnny Lazia, the crime boss, who agreed to provide them with a safe haven in exchange for cash and future consideration. Lazia and James "Jimmy Needles" LaCapra visited the two at a whorehouse and told them he needed them to do a job. If they would free Nash, they would be given $10,000 and could remain in Kansas City indefinitely. For free.

Later that night, according to FBI documents, Floyd and Richetti met with Verne Miller and obtained the machine guns necessary to do the job. They were informed that the FBI agents and local cops guarding Nash would be armed only with pistols and shotguns.

On the morning of June 17, 1933, Miller, Floyd, and Richetti entered the Union Station. Floyd and Richetti had never seen Nash and were counting on Miller to be able to identify him.

The *Little Rock Flyer* chugged into the station shortly after 7:00 a.m. Federal agents Joe Lackey and Frank Smith led Nash off the train, followed by McAllister, Oklahoma, Chief of Police Otto Reed. They were met by two more FBI agents, Raymond J. Caffrey and R. E. Vetterli. The bureau had searched hard to find two honest Kansas City police officers to accompany them. The two, Frank Hermanson and W. J. "Red" Grooms, met the party at the station.

The seven lawmen and Nash, wearing a toupee and with his manacled hands covered by a handkerchief, walked through the lobby and out into the street. They moved toward two cars. The lead car was a Chevrolet. Nash was placed in the front seat. Lackey, Reed, and Smith climbed in the back, with Smith sitting in the middle, which is where prisoners usually sat.

As the lawmen were getting into the car, Floyd ran up holding a machine gun.

"Get 'em up!" he screamed. "Put 'em up! Up! Up!"

Miller and Richetti came up on the far side.

The lawmen, taken by complete surprise, stared at the three for a few long seconds. Then officer Grooms pulled a .38-caliber revolver and squeezed off two quick shots at Floyd. Witnesses claimed the gangster was hit in the shoulder. (Floyd always wore body armor in both the front and back; thus, he was not seriously wounded.)

As soon as Grooms fired, Verne Miller yelled, "Let 'em have it!"

The gangsters then blazed away with their machine guns. Hermanson's head was blasted off, and he fell dead. Grooms was cut in half and died in a pool of blood. Agent Vetterli, hit in the shoulder, ducked behind the car, then made a dash for the Union Station. He made it, and later claimed he was going for reinforcements.

Agent Caffrey fell to the pavement, hit in the temple by a shotgun slug. (It later turned out that at least two lawmen had in all probability been killed by their own in the confused gunfight.) He would later die of his wound.

Nash was heard to scream, "For God's sake, don't shoot me." A second later, his head exploded from a gun blast, sending his bloody toupee flying. Agent Lackey was hit twice but survived. Chief Reed died of multiple gunshots and fell on top of Frank Smith. The agent decided to play dead, and lay on the floor praying for the shooting to end. He was the only lawman who was not wounded. (It is thought that the gunmen assumed that Smith was Nash and did not shoot him.)

Floyd looked into the car and shouted, "They're dead. They're all dead."

Miller, whose purpose was to free Nash, cursed, then fled, followed by Floyd and Richetti. A motorcycle cop, Mike Fanning, happened on the scene and fired several shots at the fleeing men.

The trio jumped into a waiting getaway car and screeched away from the scene. Miller drove them back to his apartment where they were treated by a doctor for minor wounds, then taken to a safe house. Within two days, they had been whisked out of town.

The Kansas City Massacre, as it was called, was the death-knell for gangsterism in the United States. Even many of the poor who looked on outlaws as "Robin Hoods" turned against them. And J. Edgar Hoover became obsessed with wiping out what he saw as a threat to the American way of life.

While the FBI was gearing up to catch the perpetrators, the three assassins were running for their lives. Miller fled to Illinois, then caught a plane to New York City. He had contacts there whom he was sure would help him. Unfortunately for him, as the fallout from the massacre fell squarely on the mob, Miller made himself expendable. Outside a bar in Newark, he killed a member of Longie Zwillman's gang, then fled to Louisville. There he was caught by members of the mob and killed. In *The Life and Death of Pretty Boy Floyd*, author Jeffery S. King writes: "His naked body [was taken] hundreds of miles by car to a drainage ditch near Detroit, where they dumped his body, which was found on November 29, 1933. It was more than a routine gangland execution: clothesline bound his arms and legs; his skull had been crushed by blows with a blunt instrument; his tongue and cheeks had been punctured with ice picks; and he had burn scars on his body."

John Lazia had arranged for Floyd and Richetti to be driven out of Kansas City. They went first to St. Louis, then

Cleveland. They finally landed in Buffalo, New York, renting an apartment with their mistresses. They stayed for a year, rarely leaving the building.

Public outrage over the Kansas City Massacre, as well as several other highly publicized crimes, such as the kidnapping of Charles Lindbergh's infant son, led Congress to expand the powers of the FBI to investigate "interstate crimes" and institute heavy punishments for those convicted of assaulting or killing a federal agent.

On July 10, 1934, Johnny Lazia was murdered by members of a rival Kansas City gang. James LaCapra, aka Jimmy Needles, was also on the run after two attempts on his life. The FBI figured that would be a good time to offer him protection for his testimony before a federal grand jury. Jimmy Needles accepted and provided a detailed recreation of the plot to free Frank Nash. He told how Lazia had arranged for Miller, Floyd, and Richetti to "disappear" after the failed attempt. [Note: There are many theories which exonerate Floyd and Richetti. The authors have used the prevailing data, which points to them.]

After the grand jury hearing, in which other witnesses and physical evidence corroborated LaCapra's testimony, the FBI announced that Pretty Boy Floyd was "public enemy number one." From that point on, Floyd and Richetti would be too hot for the mob.

A few months after testifying, LaCapra's body was found in New York state. He'd been strafed by dozens of bullets.

In October 1934, Floyd and Richetti decided to head back to Oklahoma, the one place where people were still friendly to them and where they could hide. With the last of the money they had gotten from Lazia, they bought a new car. Taking their mistresses in tow, they began driving west.

But near East Liverpool, Ohio, they were involved in a

minor accident. There, Richetti was captured by a local police chief named John H. Fultz. Floyd escaped briefly but was tracked down and killed by FBI agents and local lawmen. (Hoover's edict of "shoot to kill" was no more prevalent than here—Floyd never fired a shot and was running away. He was hit by three bullets in the back and one in the arm.)

Richetti was returned to Kansas City where he was tried for the murder of the two police officers. On June 17, 1935, he was convicted and sentenced to die.

After numerous appeals, just past midnight on October 6, 1938, Richetti was led kicking and screaming to the brand-new gas chamber in the Missouri State Prison at Jefferson City. He screamed over and over that he was innocent. "Why are you doing this to me?" he kept asking the guards.

When he was strapped into the chair in the center of the execution chamber, he held his breath. At 12:10 a.m., cyanide "eggs" were dumped into a bucket of water, and fumes began to spew into the chamber. Richetti gasped loudly, swallowed, then collapsed in the chair. At 12:14, he was pronounced dead by the prison doctor.

By the time Richetti died, most of the notorious gangsters of the Prohibition era had been eliminated. John Dillinger, Baby Face Nelson, Pretty Boy Floyd, Bonnie and Clyde, and the Barker Gang were dead and buried. Alvin "Old Creepy" Karpis was in prison.

When Eddie Richetti died a miserable coward's death in Missouri's gas chamber, he symbolized the end of an era.

Train Man

I note by the attached newspaper clipping that one of the two train robbers killed while attempting to hold up a train on the Southern Pacific Railway on the 15th . . . has been identified as Ben Kilpatrick.

— Letter from the Postal Inspector,
March 16, 1912

Ben Kilpatrick was a career criminal. He wasn't particularly good at his chosen profession, train robbery. But as long as he remained with the Hole in the Wall Gang of Butch Cassidy and the Sundance Kid, his shortcomings were masked.

Kilpatrick was born in Concho County, Texas, in 1874. He left home while still a child. Arthur Soule, in his book *The Tall Texan: The Story of Ben Kilpatrick*, writes that although "Ben had little schooling, he was not illiterate. According to Jim Pharis, a local who knew Ben, he had a great ability to do the fancy writing of the day, complete with the flourishes and curly cues."

By the time he was fourteen, Kilpatrick was working on a cattle ranch in Howard County, northwest of San Angelo. Despite his youth, he became a keen appraiser of horseflesh.

Between jobs, he would visit his family back at the Concho County ranch.

Several years later, Kilpatrick was still working as a cowboy in West Texas. Now, though, he was a top hand. He'd learned to read a compass, live off the land, fight with his bare knuckles, and shoot a firearm. His services were sought after by many of the large ranches in West Texas, where he was reputed to be unsurpassed in his working with horses.

For some reason, Kilpatrick decided to go looking for greener pastures. He crossed the Pecos River and then the Texas border and soon found himself wrangling cattle for the Diamond A Ranch near Rodeo, New Mexico. Already working there were two brothers, Tom and Sam Ketchum.

Like Kilpatrick, the Ketchums were tall, powerful men, each said to stand at least six feet four and weigh more than 200 pounds. But other than size and a propensity to take other peoples' money, the brothers had little in common. Sam was a warm-hearted and impulsive fellow, red-faced and burly, who often greeted an acquaintance with a big grin, a slap on the shoulder, and a blast of last night's whiskey.

Tom Ketchum, who later took the moniker "Black Jack," was belligerent and boisterous. His moods ranged from merely frosty to downright hostile, and he had a fondness for violence. His first encounter with the law was in 1888 and was reported in the *San Angelo Standard Times*. While riding through San Angelo, he was irritated by the barking of a dog, which he promptly shot dead. Just as promptly, he was arrested by the local constable and thrown into jail for disturbing a church service.

By 1893, the Ketchums were fully focused armed robbers. Their territory was mostly eastern New Mexico, a blistering environment that was scarcely populated and almost entirely unregulated. In that rugged terrain, the sun blazed hot by day, and the dry-country cold bit very hard at night.

The surface of the land was strewn with flint and black lava. Creosote bushes, chaparral, and beargrass competed with unquenchable cactus for the available water, and it took several acres to feed a single cow.

Somewhere within those immeasurable miles that comprised the Diamond A Ranch, middle-aged Tom Ketchum chanced upon young Ben Kilpatrick. Ben, whose disposition was similar to Sam Ketchum's, was stirred by the boastings of the psychopathic Tom. Kilpatrick soon quit his fifty-dollar-a-month wrangling job and cast his lot with Black Jack Ketchum. Ben must have wanted his chance at fame and fortune and the good life that came with them. What Black Jack didn't share with his protégé was the fact that riding the outlaw trail meant living close to death. For those who chose to become outlaws, the odds of being suddenly added to the list of the late lamented were extremely high.

Riding with Tom and Sam Ketchum consisted mostly of sitting around in the caves and caverns that dotted southeastern New Mexico. Arthur Soule believes that Ben served his apprenticeship under the Ketchums as a logistics specialist. Such tasks as scouting the target to be robbed and obtaining adequate horseflesh for the getaways demanded that the scout be unknown to local lawmen and the general public. Kilpatrick had not been linked to any gangs or robberies and thus was free to travel the expansive areas of New Mexico and Arizona without attracting much attention. Post offices, general stores, banks, and trains were what he scouted, since those were what the Ketchums tended to rob.

Kilpatrick was connected with the Black Jack Ketchum Gang from 1893 until its decline in 1898. He actively participated in at least eight robberies, but his identity remained unknown to law enforcement officials and reporters. Along the way, he met and established a friendship with Butch Cassidy and members of the Hole in the Wall Gang.

But Pinkerton agents and railroad detectives had cast a net around that fabled band of robbers and were drawing it tight. If someone entered a bank anywhere in the West and presented a large bill or bearer bond (these were rare in the region and mostly transported between banks by train) a Pinkerton agent would show up soon after.

And wherever a sighting of Cassidy, Harry Longabaugh, or Harvey Logan was reported, a skinny man with a huge 8-gauge shotgun would soon arrive and begin interviewing witnesses. Charlie Siringo was a railroad detective with an almost unlimited access to funds with which to buy information and hire private posses. A more tenacious manhunter probably never existed, and for ten years Siringo's sole mission was to hound Cassidy and Longabaugh until he captured them, killed them, or ran them off the American continent.

In 1898, the banished Hole in the Wallers migrated to New Mexico and got jobs herding cows for the W S Ranch near Alma. Their intention was to lay low for a year or two, then pull one more big robbery and filter back into society as law-abiding citizens.

Meanwhile, in southeastern New Mexico, things were falling apart for the Black Jack Ketchum Gang. Tom had never been accused of being coherent or organized, but by the spring of '98, he had become utterly unglued. For some reason known only to himself, he decided he was entitled to 50 percent of any future proceeds from robberies in which he participated. He also had noted that the other gang members had begun to look to his brother Sam for guidance. Tom and Sam quarreled, and Tom "Black Jack" Ketchum rode off in a huff for Arizona.

Sam Ketchum, hulking and affable, was a capable follower but a disaster as a gang leader. He was obsessed with robbing the Colorado & Southern's *Texas Fast Flyer* again, even though the gang had robbed it the year before. Ben Kilpatrick, who had handled the horse relay in the '97 robbery, thought the idea was preposterous. He and Sam Ketchum parted amicably, then Kilpatrick rode off to Alma, where he knew Cassidy was punching cows for wages.

Kilpatrick's decision proved a wise one. Almost immediately after robbing the *Flyer*, the gang members were tracked down by a posse and killed.

Kilpatrick had always been an agreeable sort of fellow with passable manners. He was straight in his dealings with his comrades, and almost every outlaw he came across spoke highly of him to their associates. His tenure at the W S Ranch was no exception. He was soon at the center of heavy scheming and plotting being done around the campfires. The fruition of those evening sessions would become evident on June 2, 1899.

At 2:18 that morning, in middle of a hard rain, the Union Pacific Overland Limited Express Train No. 1 was robbed west of Wilcox, Wyoming, by at least two men wearing masks. The safe was blown to smithereens, and according to the *Salt Lake Tribune*, $36,000 in cash and $10,000 in diamonds were taken. The word passed along the outlaw grapevine was that Longabaugh and Logan had held up the train.

Ben Kilpatrick was credited with holding the getaway replacement horses about 10 miles from where the train was robbed. The pursuing posse was quickly eluded, and the alleged bandits went back to work at the ranch. The only blemish involving the robbery was that a conductor had noticed that the blast which blew open the safe had also blown a corner off all of the bills. This observation was quickly publicized and widely circulated.

Later that year, Harry Longabaugh (also known as the Sundance Kid) was falling-down drunk in an Alma saloon. During the course of his quaffing, Longabaugh decided to buy a round for the house. He paid the bartender with a twenty-dollar bill that had a missing corner. Everybody toasted the health of the Sundance Kid. Longabaugh consumed a few more and rode back to the ranch.

Later that week, Frank Maury, the Pinkerton agency's Denver bureau chief, showed up in Alma and began asking pointed questions about some of the cowboys who worked at the W S Ranch. Word filtered back to the wranglers, and Cassidy knew that it was time to move on. Harvey Logan (aka Kid Curry), who seemed to spend most of his life either selecting people he would like to kill or actually killing them, voted to assassinate Maury. Butch Cassidy nixed that idea, and he and Sundance headed west to the Hole in the Wall. Kilpatrick and Logan moseyed down to Texas.

Ben Kilpatrick remained out of sight for the remainder of 1899 and throughout 1900. Historians believe that during this period he was involved in several robberies with Harvey Logan, but there is no consensus about what or where they supposedly struck. Biographer Soule thinks that Ben was present at the morbid hanging of Black Jack Ketchum. Soule writes, "Some old timers around Clayton report a well-dressed man showed up at the execution. Tom [i.e., Black Jack] was said to have made a definite eye contact with the person before the black hood was placed over his head. After the trap was sprung, the man quickly left. The old timers think that man was Ben Kilpatrick."

It well might have been. Tom Ketchum had been Kilpatrick's first mentor, and Ben Kilpatrick was heralded as a staunch supporter of his friends. However, if he truly did witness the execution, it failed to make a lasting impression on him.

On the afternoon of July 3, 1901, the Hole in the Wall Gang as a group pulled its last job. Ben Kilpatrick was riding with them.

The gang robbed the Great Northern Express Train near Malta, Montana. They got $41,500 in incomplete bank notes. (The bank notes looked like currency, but were not government bills. The difference was that they were distributed by local banks. If they were incomplete, the signatures of the president of the bank and other officials were not present.)

Most of the bills from the Malta robbery were drawn on the National Bank of Helena. Since they had no signatures, Ben Kilpatrick was assigned to forge them.

By all accounts, his forgeries were masterpieces. Unfortunately for him and the gang, anytime a Bank of Helena bill showed up, Pinkerton agents were right behind. After the robbery, Kilpatrick and his longtime girlfriend, Laura Bullion, made their way back to Texas. The easily identifiable bills began popping up all over West Texas, including Fort Worth and San Antonio. Seemingly oblivious to the net that was closing in on them, Kilpatrick and Bullion leisurely left Texas and went on a spending spree throughout the Midwest.

On November 1, 1901, the lovers registered at the Laclede Hotel in St. Louis. Over the next several days, Kilpatrick purchased clothes, a pocket watch, whiskey, and other luxury items. A local barber, however, recognized several of the Bank of Helena bills and alerted the police. It wasn't long before the Secret Service was called.

On November 5, Kilpatrick was arrested at a "house of prostitution." It was reported that he was in the company of several girls. Three handguns were found in his clothes, but the outlaw had no chance to get to them. Laura Bullion was arrested when she left the hotel to go looking for her lover. Authorities recovered nearly $8,000 in stolen bills from the pair.

They were charged with seventeen counts of forgery, counterfeiting, and passing forged obligations. After a month of legal wrangling, each defendant pleaded guilty to one count of unlawfully possessing national bank notes. Laura was sentenced to five years in prison.

Kilpatrick was sentenced to fifteen years at hard labor, most of which he would serve in the federal penitentiary at Atlanta.

Ben Kilpatrick was not a model prisoner. In an era where pardons, parole, and probation were handed out like candy,

Kilpatrick served more than ten years of his sentence. By contrast, Laura was released after serving less than eighteen months.

While in prison, Kilpatrick met another counterfeiter, Ole Beck (also known as Ole Hobek). Beck's specialty was counterfeiting silver dollars. He had been arrested and convicted numerous times but always seemed to receive short sentences. In 1907, Beck was forty-three years old when he was arrested again. This time he was sentenced to three years at hard labor and shipped to the federal penitentiary in Atlanta to serve out his sentence. Beck and Kilpatrick were probably cellmates as well as friends. As usual, Beck served slightly more than a year of his sentence, then was paroled.

After years of bucking the system, the hard-case Kilpatrick finally saw the light. He realized that the way to get out early was to appear to have been reformed. To that end, he stopped complaining, and made a public display of reading the Bible.

It worked. He was finally released June 11, 1911.

David Trousdale was the opposite of Kilpatrick and Beck. He'd worked hard for a living all his life. Born in Columbia, Tennessee, he'd left in 1900 to begin punching cattle in Hutto, Texas. In 1903, according to Soule:

> [Trousdale] became an employee of Wells, Fargo in San Antonio on December 1, 1903, performing duties as a clerk. He transferred to the company's road service on April 24, 1906, serving as a helper on the Southern Pacific between San Antonio and Spoffard. He next served three and a half years on the Gulf, Colorado & Santa Fe, his run traveling between Somerville and Beaumont, Texas. The

year 1910 found him back in San Antonio, on the San Antonio & Aransas Pass. . . . Prior to the robbery he was transferred to the San Antonio and El Paso run."

On the evening of March 12, 1912, Trousdale was performing his duties as express messenger of the GC&SF No. 9 train near Dryden, Texas. The train was running late, and a lone fireman sweated as he stoked the engine's boiler. Black smoke belched from the stack and disappeared into the night.

Trousdale was in the forward passenger car when two men stepped through the door and trained their guns on him. He noticed that one was tall, the other short. The tall robber would later be identified as Ben Kilpatrick; the shorter man was Ole Beck.

"Anybody left in the forward cars?" asked Kilpatrick. Trousdale hesitated. The robber angrily pointed his rifle at him. Finally, Trousdale said, "One of our helpers is in the head combination car."

The men forced Trousdale into the combination mail car and baggage car. When they entered, the helper, a man named Reagan, was searched for weapons. Other employees were gathered and searched.

Reagan, mail clerk Banks, and Trousdale were then ordered by the robbers into the locomotive's cab. There, Kilpatrick held his gun on the engineer and ordered him to stop the train.

As it chugged to a halt, Kilpatrick forced Trousdale, Reagan, and Banks back into the combination car. Beck, holding a revolver, stayed in the cab with the other railroad employees.

Once they entered the baggage car, the tall robber pulled a knife from his coat and began slicing the straps of the mail pouches. He searched the contents, placed certain items into a bag, and threw the remaining pouches out the window.

The robber then ordered Trousdale and Reagan to go to the express car. Kilpatrick followed, still holding the rifle on the employees. As they entered the car's cramped quarters, Trousdale passed an ice box. The robber turned his attention to the safe, allowing the messenger express agent to pick up a mallet used for chipping ice. He stuck the maul in his pocket and covered it with his overcoat.

"Open the safe!" the robber ordered.

Trousdale knelt down and clicked the combination lock until the door opened. There was little inside it; the robber got thirty-seven dollars.

Trousdale, thinking fast, pointed to a package the robber had missed.

Kilpatrick set the rifle on his lap and reached inside the safe. As he was bent over, Trousdale pulled the mallet from his pocket and smashed the robber in the head. Kilpatrick went down in a heap.

Trousdale hit him twice more.

Blood and brains spattered the car.

Trousdale waited a few minutes to make sure Kilpatrick was dead, then moved over and took the robber's gun, which turned out to be a Model 1910 Winchester .401-caliber rifle. The agent also found two .45-caliber Colt revolvers in the outlaw's pockets.

Trousdale handed Reagan and Banks the revolvers and told them to guard the rear of the car.

He then turned out the lights and waited. In the silence, he wondered about the second robber. Was he still in the cab? Were there other robbers? Was the robber on the floor dead? The man had moaned once or twice after Trousdale hit him but had made no sound since.

After what seemed like an eternity, Trousdale decided to try to draw the short robber out. He fired a shot through the roof of the express car. Then he waited. A few minutes later, he heard a commotion outside. The robber appeared at the window. Then he slowly entered the car. He ducked behind a trunk, then raised his head to look around.

Trousdale, sitting in the darkness, could see the man's silhouette against the window. He aimed and fired. The robber fell into the car. Later, a medical examiner would determine that Beck had been shot through the left eye.

Again, Trousdale waited. Again, it seemed like an eternity. Finally, he edged along the boxes, keeping out of sight, until he reached the robber. The man was dead.

Trousdale took a .380-caliber semiautomatic pistol from Beck. He also found a bottle filled with nitroglycerine. Searching Kilpatrick again, he found six sticks of dynamite and a detonator.

Trousdale ordered employees to pick up the mail bags that had been thrown out the window. Then the train proceeded to Sanderson, Texas, and law enforcement officers were notified.

Once the robbers were identified, it was determined that they were suspects in numerous small-time robberies that had occurred since they'd been released from prison.

The world had changed since Ben Kilpatrick first entered prison. Telephones now connected cities across America, and motorcars had replaced horses in most towns.

Another thing that had changed directly affected Kilpatrick's profession. Trains no longer carried large payrolls. He had no way of knowing it, but his latest robberies had been doomed from the start. In at least two train robberies they'd committed since being released, Kilpatrick and Beck had collected less than a thousand dollars.

The day after the attempted robbery, a posse was formed and began a search of the area near Baxter's Curve, where the attempted robbery had occurred. It is probable that many posse members drove to the scene in motorcars. The lawmen found three horses a few miles from the scene of the robbery. Two were already saddled, and the third carried supplies. All the horses were shoed backwards, tied to stakes in the ground, and had bags over their heads. Many historians suspect that Laura Bullion tended the horses while Kilpatrick and Beck tried to rob the train. She was known to have been in the area and then quickly left. What happened to her after that is unknown—the girlfriend of Ben Kilpatrick disappeared from the history books.

Ben Kilpatrick, the Tall Texan, and Ole Beck were buried at county expense in Sanderson. Their graves overlooked the railroad track where, for many years thereafter, the *Texas Fast Flyer* would chug by on its appointed route.

For his part, Trousdale received a reward of $1,000 from Wells Fargo. The Southern Pacific also paid him $500 for killing the two robbers. Passengers on the train took up a collection and purchased a gold watch for him.

After taking a long vacation and visiting his family in Tennessee, Trousdale continued his work as an express agent for Wells Fargo.

Final Solution

*When everything else fails, I have a solution
which never does.*

— Tom Horn, at a meeting with
Wyoming Governor William A. Richards, 1895

A few minutes before seven o'clock on the morning of
July 18, 1901, fourteen-year-old Willie Nickell saddled
his father's horse. The Nickell family lived on a farm about
thirty miles north of Cheyenne, Wyoming, in an area called
Iron Mountain. That morning, a heavy fog blanketed the
mountains surrounding the family home, but Willie Nickell
didn't mind. He was proud to have been given an important
job by his father.

Instead of his own pony, he'd been ordered to take his
father's more durable horse. Within a few minutes, this
switch would have fatal consequences for the boy.

The day before, a stranger had ridden up to the ranch
and asked Kels Nickell if he had an opening for an experienced sheep herder. When Kels informed him that he
already had a herder, the man had thanked him and

galloped away. Kels watched him head south, then went back to work.

That night, his own herder, John Scroder, told Kels that he was quitting. Kels tried to talk Scroder out of it, but the man was adamant. Kels then called his son into the room and instructed him to leave at daybreak and trail the job-seeker. When he was found, Willie was to offer the man a job.

At exactly seven o'clock, the teen mounted the horse and headed toward a gate nearly a mile from the house. By now, the fog had settled into the valley, obscuring the scraggly trees and rocky crags along the trail. As he rode along, Willie heard the growling waters of Chugwater Creek which ran beside the trail.

When he reached the gate, Willie dismounted and unhitched a wire loop from two posts. The boy had trained his own horse to stand parallel to the fence so that he could bend down and remove the loop. But because his father's horse was unable to perform the trick, Willie had to step down to do it.

He opened the gate and walked through it, leading the horse by the reins. As he turned back to replace the loop, a shot rang out of the fog.

Willie was hit in the back. The boy tried to remain standing, but a second shot knocked him to the ground. A third shot missed him. Willie staggered to his feet and began to lurch back toward the ranch. Gasping for air and leaving a grotesque blood trail, the boy managed to run sixty-five yards before collapsing. He was already dead when the killer walked out of the fog and turned the body over on its back. He may have cursed to himself—Willie Nickell wasn't the person he'd intended to kill. Blood soaked the front of Willie's clothes. A coroner's report would later show that he'd been hit in the back by two rounds from a .30-30 rifle. One bullet had exited through the sternum, the other had ripped through the abdomen.

The boy's corpse lay near the gate for a day and a half. When he didn't return on the night of the eighteenth, his family assumed he'd had trouble locating the drifter and had spent the night with friends.

On the following day, Willie's younger brother Freddie rode by the gate to round up stray cattle. Finding Willie's body, the boy ran screaming to the house.

Kels Nickell, along with several family members and hired hands, raced to the site. When they arrived and saw the bloated corpse, they were distraught.

After hauling the body back to the house in a wagon, Kels Nickell sent a rider to Cheyenne. On Saturday, July 20, Deputy Sheriff Peter Warlaumont arrived at the farm with a coroner and stenographer. By the time they arrived, little evidence remained at the scene of the murder.

Kels related what had happened. When he came to the spot, he said, Kels found Willie on his back with a rock underneath his head. When asked by the sheriff who he thought had committed the murder, Nickell stated, "Jim Miller. But they'll blame it on Tom Horn." He added that he and Miller, his neighbor, had been feuding for years.

The distraught father stated that he and several friends had canvassed the area of the shooting but could find no tracks because a herd of cattle had tromped out of the open gate. A large rock about thirty feet away from the gate may have been where the killer had stood. There was another outcropping about 300 yards away but it was thought that no one could make such a shot, especially in the heavy fog.

When Nickell mentioned Tom Horn's name, alarm bells went off in Sheriff Warlaumont's mind. Though he'd never been convicted of any murders, Horn was suspected of being an assassin for the Wyoming cattle barons. The lawman asked the grieving father why he thought Horn would be blamed for the murder. "Well," Nickell replied, "he spent the last week at the Millers' ranch."

Sheriff Warlaumont arranged for a coroner's hearing to be held the following day. District Attorney Walter Stoll was brought in to conduct the questioning.

Jim Miller was one of the first witnesses called to testify. He denied having any knowledge of the murder but conceded that he and Nickell had been feuding for years. One of the reasons, according to Miller's testimony, was because Nickell had imported 3,000 head of sheep and let them graze on his (Miller's) land. Miller maintained, as did most cattlemen, that sheep stripped the land, leaving cattle without food. He described Kels as irrational, and stated under oath that his neighbor had threatened many times to "whip" Miller's sons, or worse, kill them. The feud had become so intense that both sides had begun carrying guns wherever they went.

Indeed, that had led to a tragic shooting. The accident was later described in a journal by Mrs. Nettie Jordan, a neighbor of the Millers. "One morning," she wrote, "Mr. Miller took two of his children with him in the spring wagon [when] he was going to cut hay. The children were playing and the gun accidentally went off and shot both children." Fourteen-year-old Frank Miller died of his wounds, and ten-year-old Maude had part of her face shot off. Although she survived, Maude was scarred for the rest of her life.

Jim Miller blamed the shooting on Kels. He reasoned that if Nickell hadn't forced him to carry a gun everywhere, the shooting would not have occurred. According to several witnesses, Miller threatened to take revenge on his irascible neighbor.

A few days after the inquest, Sheriff Warlaumont arrested Jim Miller and two of his sons, Gus and Victor. They were taken to the Cheyenne jail and interrogated. The three were quickly released, however, when it was proven beyond doubt that they were at home when the killing occurred. Indeed, they'd held a dance the night before which had lasted deep into the night—several of their guests had stayed over and eaten breakfast with the suspects the following morning.

One man who'd been in the area, however, had no such alibi. His name was Tom Horn.

At the time of Willie Nickell's murder, Tom Horn's name was whispered among residents of the Iron Mountain area as being the killer. It certainly had all the earmarks of another Horn murder. But Sheriff Warlaumont and his deputies were unable to prove it.

Horn was already a legend. He'd been a cowboy, a lawman, a rodeo star, a respected detective for Pinkerton's Detective Agency, and a military hero. Indeed, he'd been chief of scouts for the U.S. Army when they captured the great Apache chief Geronimo. Later, he accompanied Theodore Roosevelt to Cuba during the Spanish-American War.

As a detective, Horn had an uncanny ability to track fugitives for hundreds of miles. He was one of the few truly effective agents that Pinkerton employed.

But a dark side of his personality kept popping up.

While working for Pinkerton, he was accused of robbing a faro dealer in Reno, Nevada. The first trial ended with a hung jury. Horn was acquitted after a second trial, but the embarrassment to the Pinkerton Agency was profound.

On another occasion, a drunken Horn instigated a barroom fight in which he was knocked unconscious. While on the floor, his opponent pulled a knife and slit his throat. It took Horn months to recuperate, and the knife wound left a large ugly scar. As soon as he was able to ride, however, Horn tracked down his nemesis and murdered him.

In yet another saloon fight, Horn tangled with a semiprofessional boxer named Johnny "Young" Corbett. Not surprisingly, Horn ended up with a broken jaw and another long stay in the hospital.

When he was drinking, Horn was an obnoxious braggart and bully. When he was sober, he could be charming, cultured, and an entertaining conversationalist.

It is not known exactly when Horn committed his first murder. Nor is it known exactly how many men he killed.

Tom Horn was born in Missouri in 1860. He left home when he was thirteen and headed west. He is known to have been in Wyoming as early as 1892. A friend, John C. Coble, co-owner of the Iron Mountain Ranch Company, hired Horn to help stop the rustling of his cattle. Later, Horn was hired by the Swan Land & Cattle Company in Chugwater. Initially, his job was to obtain evidence that could be used in court to prosecute rustlers.

The cattle industry had its start in Wyoming shortly after the Civil War. About a dozen settlers began ranching north of Cheyenne. In addition to hundreds of thousands of acres which they owned, the cattlemen also grazed their herds on open land. But in the 1880s and 1890s, small farmers began buying up the open range. Most of these newcomers owned 300 acres or less.

Conflict between the two groups was inevitable. Tensions were heightened even further when a few of the "nesters" began rustling cattle from the large cattlemen. According to Chip Carlson, in his book *Tom Horn: Blood on the Moon*:

> The Johnson County War, launched in April 1892, was an effort by large cattlemen to solve what they perceived as their major problem: rustling in central Wyoming. The failed effort involved gunmen hired from Texas and a special train from Denver that surreptitiously picked up the cattlemen in Cheyenne. The cattlemen's intent was to murder or drive out all the suspected rustlers and install their own politicians to power.
>
> From Cheyenne they proceeded to Casper, where they disembarked and continued north via

horseback and wagon toward Buffalo. They side-tracked to Kaycee, where they murdered Nick Ray and Nate Campion. The delay allowed their adversaries to learn of the foray, organize, and advance toward the south from Buffalo. The cattlemen's expedition ended with a gunfight when locals surrounded the invaders at the TA ranch.

Tom Horn wasn't involved in this fiasco, but his unique skills would soon be in demand.

Horn patrolled the Big Horn country for the cattlemen. In early 1894, he caught four members of the Langhoff family red-handed as they were butchering rustled cattle at night. Arresting the perpetrators, Horn and Al Bowie, another stock detective, escorted the captives to Cheyenne.

To the disappointment of the Wyoming Cattlemen's Association, three of the alleged rustlers weren't even charged and the fourth was given a light sentence. This hardened the resolve of the cattlemen to use any means necessary to eliminate the nesters once and for all.

In 1895, Governor W. A. Richards, who was also one of the large ranchers, met with Tom Horn to discuss how to get rid of the hated enemy. According to a witness, Horn cut to the chase. "I have a system that never fails," he said. "Yours has."

Shortly after the meeting, nesters began dying. Typically, a hand-written note would arrive at the home of a suspected rustler. He would be threatened with death if he didn't pack up and leave. Initially, the settlers ignored these warnings.

The first to die was William Lewis, an Englishman suspected of rustling. He was ambushed and hit by three shots from a .30-30 rifle.

Another victim, Fred U. Powell, had been in trouble with the law since he was a teenager. He made no bones about being a rustler, even inviting the wealthy cattlemen to his humble cabin to eat their own beef. He was ambushed and murdered at his ranch.

Matt Rash and Isam Dart were also gunned down when they refused to leave the area. They were known cattle thieves.

Horn is thought to have killed at least one man by mistake. The farmer's bones were found in the desert, and he was identified by a ring he always wore. Horn was seen following the victim, and a .30-30 round was found underneath the skeleton.

By now, Tom Horn was suspected of being the assassin of these and nearly a dozen other men. Before he died, Rash had written part of Horn's name in blood on the floor of his cabin. But lawmen lacked hard evidence proving that Horn had murdered the men.

As the most feared man in Wyoming, Horn used his notoriety to intimidate suspected rustlers. He bragged about his many murders, probably exaggerating the number of people he killed. Exaggeration or not, Horn was always well-paid, and he had friends in high places.

That is, until Willie Nickell died.

Six months had passed and law enforcement hadn't been able to bring anyone to justice. In the meantime, yet another unsolved shooting had stunned the community. Kels Nickell was shot three times from ambush. Though his wounds weren't serious, he gave in, sold off his sheep, and moved his family to Cheyenne.

From the beginning, Deputy U.S. Marshal Joe LeFors had suspected Horn of the Nickell murder. His problem was how to prove it. He came up with an idea. He'd get Horn to confess in front of witnesses.

Early in 1902, LeFors contacted Horn and told the stock detective he had a job for him. On January 11, Horn met the lawman in Cheyenne. Charles Ohnhaus and Deputy Sheriff Les Snow were witnesses. In fact, Ohnhaus was a stenographer and had been assigned to record the

conversation verbatim. Horn, who'd been drinking all
night, immediately began bragging about the murders
he'd committed. LeFors guided the conversation to the
Willie Nickell killing.

"Tom," he said. "You are the best man to cover up a trail
I ever saw. In the Willie Nickell killing, I could never find
your trail, and I pride myself on being a trailer."

"I left no trail," Horn replied. "The only way to cover up
your trail is to go barefooted."

After questioning the hazards of going barefoot on rocky
ground, Lefors said, "I never knew why Willie Nickell was
killed. . . ."

"I think it went this way," Horn replied. "Suppose a man
was in the big draw to the right of the gate—you know
where it is—the draw that comes into the main creek
below Nickell's house where Nickell was shot. Well, I suppose a man was in that, and the kid came riding up on him
from this way, and suppose the kid started to run for the
house, and the fellow headed him off at the gate and killed
him to keep him from going to the house and raising a big
commotion. . . ."

LeFors, acting incredulous, asked, "Tom, you had your
boots on when you ran across there to cut the kid off, didn't
you?"

Horn was adamant. "No," he replied. "I was barefooted."

"You didn't run across there barefooted?"

"Yes, I did."

LeFors asked, "How did you get your boots on after cutting your feet?"

Horn smiled. "I generally have ten days to rest after a job
of that kind," he said.

After more banter, LeFors asked, "How far [away] was
Willie Nickell [when he was] killed?"

"About three hundred yards," Horn said. "It was the best
shot that I ever made and the dirtiest trick I ever done. . . ."

After still more conversation, LeFors asked, "Why did

you put the rock under the kid's head after you killed him. That is one of your marks, isn't it?"

Horn replied, "Yes, that is the way I hang out my sign to collect money for a job of this kind."

LeFors zeroed in on the drunken braggart. "Have you got your money yet for the killing of Nickell?" he asked.

"I got that before I did the job."

"You got five hundred dollars for that," Lefors said.

"Why did you cut the price?"

Horn replied, "I got twenty-one hundred dollars."

"How much is that a man?"

"That is for three dead men and one man shot at five times. Killing men is my specialty. I look at it as a business proposition, and I think I have a corner on the market." Stenographer Ohnhaus spent the night transcribing his shorthand. These notes would be used in the sensational trial to follow.

Sheriff Ed Smalley arrested Horn the following day. Publicly, the cattle barons began to distance themselves from Horn. Privately, they hired a crack team of experienced attorneys to defend the accused murderer.

The trial began on October 10, 1902, and lasted two weeks. Against the wishes of his lawyers, Horn took the stand. His own testimony convicted him. He came across to jurors as arrogant. He countered the statements attributed to him by contending that because he was drunk, he shouldn't be held accountable for his comments. Perhaps worst of all, the jaded gunman showed a total contempt for the rule of law. The prosecutor guided him into admitting that he was within a few miles of the Nickell homestead on the morning of the murder, and ballistics (as primitive as they were) allegedly proved that the bullet came from a rifle similar to the one Horn was known to carry.

The defense attempted to prove that Horn was twenty-five or more miles away at the time of Willie Nickell's murder. They also questioned the truthfulness of Ohnhaus and the lawmen who'd set Horn up.

This first-day cover commemorative, issued in 2003, celebrated the life of Tom Horn.

In the end, jurors found Horn guilty of first-degree murder and sentenced him to hang.

The final word on the trial may have been spoken by his frustrated attorney who said, "He talked too much."

A series of appeals followed, none of which were successful. As appeal after appeal failed, Horn realized he was doomed. While in the Cheyenne jail, he penned his autobiography and plotted an escape.

On the morning of August 9, 1903, Cheyenne was teeming with excitement as citizens prepared for the "Frontier Days" celebration. The streets were filled with a weird assortment of horses, motorcars, and bicycles. Businesses opened early and closed at midnight. Sidewalks teemed with locals and visitors.

According to *Tom Horn, Last of the Bad Men*, a semifictional account of the life of Horn, "A merry-go-round man with a calliope set up his display on a concession across from the jail. The first tune or two pleased Tom and he whistled and sang along with the organ. After a day or two, he loathed the thin, shrill music that started . . . at nine in the morning and lasted until midnight."

Inmates were housed in a series of upstairs rooms. Two rows of bars held the prisoners. The outer row stood several feet in front of the inside tier of bars. In order to reach the prisoners, the lawmen had to climb a series of steel steps, then use a key to open the outer tier of bars. The inner row of bars was opened with a remote control device.

Shortly before eight o'clock in the morning, an inmate named "Driftwood" Jim McCloud complained of stomach pains. McCloud, who shared a cell with Horn, was also suspected of being an assassin for the Wyoming cattle barons. Before hiring on with the cattlemen, his specialty had been safecracking.

The jail physician prescribed a mixture of medication and warm water for McCloud. Deputy Sheriff Dick Proctor dutifully brought the medicine and a cup of water. He unlocked the iron bars on the outer tier of the cell and walked toward the cell that housed McCloud and Horn.

According to Carlson, "Proctor found his two charges sitting on a bench on the catwalk. He opened another door that provided access to the catwalk and reached in to hand the water to McCloud. At that, both prisoners sprang and pinned Proctor's arm between the door and the jam.

"The three struggled ferociously, with Proctor at one point lifting McCloud and nearly throwing him over the railing to the concrete floor on the lower level. Horn, however, had a stranglehold around Proctor's neck, and he was forced to relent."

After choking the lawman nearly to death, Horn and McCloud tied his hands with window cord. Then they forced him to walk back down the stairs to the sheriff's office. The convicts searched the room for weapons, and McCloud located a rifle.

Outside, Deputy Les Snow had been sitting on the sidewalk with his dog. A few minutes after eight, he got up and walked slowly toward the jail.

Inside, the desperados had untied Proctor's hands so that the lawman could unlock a combination safe that contained guns and ammunition. Proctor delayed, pretending to be so nervous that he could not get the safe unlocked. McCloud placed the barrel of the rifle against the deputy's head and snarled, "If you don't open that safe, and quick, I'll kill you." A few seconds later, the safe popped open.

Proctor then asked McCloud to get a key from the desk so that he could open the inner door of the safe. As the outlaw turned toward the desk, Proctor reached into the safe and pulled out a .45-caliber semiautomatic pistol. He turned to fire at the outlaws, but Horn was too fast for him. The convict grabbed Proctor's gun hand and wrestled him to the floor. McCloud leaped onto Proctor and the three men rolled along the floor of the jail. It took several minutes to again subdue Proctor. Finally, Horn wrenched the pistol from the deputy.

Deputy Snow, who had been slowly ambling along the sidewalk, finally opened the door to jailhouse. He was met by McCloud's rifle. But instead of entering as the outlaw had invited him to do, Snow turned and ran down the street. As soon as he got a few yards from the jail, he raised his rifle into the air and began firing. The gunshots awoke many Cheyenne residents.

McCloud and Horn then ran out into the street.

McCloud ran into a nearby stable, found a horse, and began to lead it outside. Hearing the commotion, Sheriff Ed Smalley ran from his house across the street from the jail. A Cheyenne resident, Colonel A. E. Slack, yelled that one of the escapees was near the stable. Smalley raced to the stable and saw McCloud attempting to get away.

The sheriff fired three shots at the escapee. He missed, but his shots spooked the horse so that McCloud was unable to control it. The outlaw dropped the reins and ran through an alley. He turned north on Eddy Street, then ran down another alley and came out on Twenty-first Street.

On the streets, citizens had begun to assemble. Some walked while others rode horses, drove motorcars, or rode bicycles. In addition to Smalley, Proctor, and Snow, the manhunt now involved the whole town.

Pat Hennessey, a mail clerk, loaded up his double-barrel shotgun and walked outside his house. He immediately saw

McCloud coming his way. The fast-thinking convict yelled, "Tom Horn has broke out of jail. Have you seen him?"

"No," replied McCloud. "Which way did he go?"

McCloud didn't answer. Instead, he raced away. When he thought that Hennessey was out of sight, he jumped a fence and ran into a barn behind a big house.

A woman in the house saw McCloud go into the barn. She ran outside and told John Nolan, a Cheyenne police officer. Nolan and a citizen named Oscar Lamm, who was armed with a hunting rifle, came to the barn.

As Nolan tried to decide what to do, Lamm took matters into his own hands. "There he is!" he yelled. "I can kill him now!"

Although McCloud was well-hidden, he thought he'd been spotted. He hollered that he was coming out and surrendering. Sure enough, the convict walked out with his hands up.

Nolan and Lamm escorted him back to jail.

Meanwhile, Horn had wrested the semiautomatic from Proctor. After unsuccessfully attempting to shoot the deputy, he ran out the door and fled in the opposite direction of his cohort, McCloud.

As Horn ran along, he attempted to figure out how to shoot the gun. He was an expert with a revolver but was unfamiliar with the new-fangled semiautomatic firearms. Although the gun was loaded, he couldn't figure out how to release the safety.

Meanwhile, the streets were teeming with lawmen and armed citizens. A church bell began clanging—its bell sounded over and over, awakening the whole town and alerting citizens that something was wrong. Several churches were holding services, and their members ran outside to join the manhunt. Groups of neighbors gathered at various locations where word of mouth informed them of the escape of the murderer Tom Horn.

O. M. Aldrich had come to town with the fair. He was the owner of the merry-go-round whose music Horn had come to despise. As he heard the commotion outside the tent he'd set up near the jail, he grabbed a .32-caliber Iver-Johnson pistol and walked outside.

As Aldrich walked across the street, he saw Horn run around a corner. The merry-go-round operator leveled his revolver and fired. The shot missed, but he followed Horn around the corner and fired again. Horn, racing along Nineteenth Street, headed north. Leaping over fences and cutting through yards, he was just a few seconds ahead of Aldrich and several other citizens.

Suddenly, Horn stopped, turned and aimed his gun at his pursuers. He pulled the trigger, but again, the semiautomatic was locked and wouldn't fire.

Aldrich now had a clear shot.

He fired. The bullet grazed Horn's head. The impact knocked him down, but, even on the ground, the outlaw again pointed his gun at the crowd and tried to fire. He stood again and continued to pull the trigger.

As Horn attempted to shoot the ornery semiautomatic, Robert LaFontaine, who lived nearby, ran up and slammed the fugitive to the ground. Aldrich, the man who'd shot him, also joined the fray. Horn rose, still fighting. Aldrich hit Horn on the back of the head with his gun, again knocking the outlaw down. With that, several members of the crowd began beating Horn.

When police officer Otto Ahrens arrived, the bloodied Horn was glad to see him. The lawman ordered the crowd away and took Horn's gun. As the lawman arrested him, the outlaw's only words were, "Well, Otto, I guess they've got me, all right."

A troop of citizens followed as the lawman began to take Horn back to the jail. A second officer arrived and joined the escort.

At that time, Deputy Les Snow rode up on his pony. He sidled up beside Horn, then pulled his rifle from the scabbard, leaned down and tried to hit Horn with the butt. The other officers blocked the blow, and several citizens yanked Snow off his horse. They escorted the frustrated deputy back to the jail along with the prisoner.

Sheriff Ed Smalley arrived, and Horn was placed back in his cell. He and "Driftwood" Jim McCloud had tasted freedom for less than thirty minutes.

On November 20, 1903, Cheyenne was bustling with excitement. A cold wind whistled down from the mountains, but that didn't stop a large crowd from gathering. Saloons were crowded, and the streets outside were packed with men and women n heavy coats.

At eleven o'clock that morning, Tom Horn was scheduled to hang.

Cheyenne lawmen had learned their lesson. They were determined that Horn would not escape his destiny with the noose. Sheriff Smalley had obtained a Gatling gun from nearby Fort Russell and positioned it on the roof of the jail overlooking the scaffold. Dozens of lawmen from surrounding towns watched the proceedings, rifles and shotguns at the ready. Even the Wyoming militia had been called on to reinforce the lawmen.

The scaffold stood a few feet from the jail. It was a Rube Goldberg-type contraption that was designed to operate without a hangman. According to Jay Monaghan, "The trap on the scaffold was supported by a beam constructed in three sections and set upright in such a manner that, when sufficient water was released from a tank to overbalance an iron weight, it dropped and jerked out the middle of the beam. . . . The trap opened on its hinges and let the hanged man drop six feet on the end of a three-quarter inch rope. Once the trap doors had been sprung, they were restrained by weights and pulleys to prevent them from banging against the body."

Shortly before eleven, Horn was led from his cell by Sheriff Smalley and two deputies. They walked through a gauntlet of lawmen, reporters, and citizens who had been approved to view the execution.

Two men began to sing. It was an eerie duet, their a capella harmony silencing the crowd.

Life is like a mountain railroad
With an engineer that's brave.
You must make your run successful
From the cradle to the grave.

Two clergymen, a Catholic priest and a Protestant minister, led Horn up the steps to the gallows. The prisoner was an avowed atheist, but he hadn't objected when the religious men had volunteered to escort him. The voices of the singers and the chants of the priest provided an eerie backdrop to the scene.

Once Horn arrived at the top of the gallows, Smalley attached a harness to his body. The straps were designed to immobilize the prisoner. Once the harness was attached, Smalley placed a black hood on the outlaw's face. Finally, the buckskin rope was put into place around Horn's neck. "Anything you want to say, Tom?" Smalley asked.

There was no reply.

The singing was louder now, drowning out the priest's chants. The Protestant minister stood erect, his head bowed, mouthing a prayer.

The sheriff moved away.

Smalley gave a signal, and the water valve began to hiss. After an excruciating forty-five seconds, the trap door sprang. Its sharp boom caused many in the crowd to jump. Horn dangled for sixteen minutes before a doctor pronounced him dead.

John Coble, one of the cattle barons, paid for his funeral. Tom Horn was buried in the Pioneer Cemetery in Cheyenne.

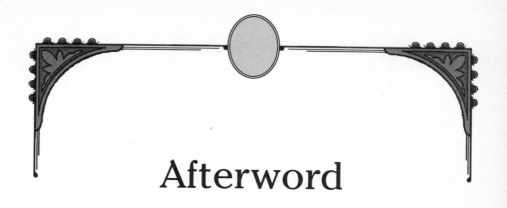

Afterword

The authors make no pretense of being professional historians, though both have studied history. However, many times outsiders bring different perspectives to issues.

Our research has shown that not enough attention has been given to the average citizens who settled this country. Recent emphasis on the early history of African-Americans, women, Orientals, and other groups has added layers of understanding to our rich culture. We hope the stories described here will focus attention on the courage exhibited by the ordinary inhabitants of the Old West and the Prohibition era.

For every outlaw, there were thousands of citizens who lived decent lives. For many, it was a struggle to survive. In an agrarian economy, jobs were hard to come by. But as settlers moved west, a market developed for teachers, ministers, clerks, editors, saloon-keepers, tailors, bankers, and many others.

As in any civilization, their views on life varied. While some glorified outlaws and gangsters, others were appalled by the murders, robberies, and mayhem perpetrated by criminals.

A deep populist strain has always existed in middle America, an ingrained suspicion of those in authority and those who control vast amounts of wealth. Instilled in this mentality is an inclination to root for the underdog. Those who looked on criminals as heroes admired the outlaw as an individualist who followed his own path. According to this line of thought, he often fought against the very people who oppressed the ordinary citizen, the banker, the railroad tycoon, even the law itself.

But the tendency to sympathize with outlaws was more abstract than concrete. When the local bank was being robbed, citizens tended to become protective of "their" own. There was a strong sense of outrage that outsiders would come into a community and try to take what wasn't theirs. Call it a sense of fairness.

Even so, citizens could sometimes be bought by out-laws. Especially in rural areas, where no protection from law enforcement existed. In a bleak land with bleak prospects, it was easy to shelter a stranger who paid generously, and it was easy to rationalize that the cash being handed over was not bribe money but was taken from an evil banker who would foreclose in a heartbeat.

But deep down almost everyone, including the criminals, knew that robbery and murder were sins against man and God. In the heartland, strong religious beliefs conflicted with any tendency to absolve those who broke the law.

It is safe to say that one or more churches sprang up in every community. Moral values were instilled in children at an early age. Virtues such as honesty, hard work, and sym-pathy for the less fortunate were taught to most youngsters.

Which brings us to one of the most brutal thugs to ever roam the Old West. "Deacon Jim" Miller used religion to cloak a murderous reign that continued for two decades. In 1909, as he was being strung up by the enraged citizens of Ada, Oklahoma, he is said to have admitted to having assassinated fifty-one men.

During his reign of terror, James B. Miller perfected the art of murder as well the art of avoiding conviction. While most people knew he was guilty of the crimes, he was convicted only once, and that conviction was overturned on appeal.

Miller, born in Arkansas in 1866, attended church regularly. He made it a point to let people see him dropping wads of cash into the collection plate. And he displayed an outward piousness that appealed to Christians.

But Deacon Jim was a born killer.

When he was eight years old, he was arrested for gunning down his own grandparents. In those days, as today, law enforcement had few answers for children who killed. Miller was sent to live with his sister and brother-in-law in Coryell County, Texas. It was widely known that Miller hated John Coop, his sister's husband, because the farmer insisted that the youngster pull his share of work on the family spread. One night, when Miller was eighteen, Coop was killed by a shotgun blast as he sat on his front porch.

Miller was the only suspect, but he swore under oath that he'd been at a local camp meeting when the crime occurred. No witnesses could vouch for him, however, and strong circumstantial evidence pointed to him as the perpetrator. He was tried and convicted, but the verdict was overturned on appeal.

Miller fled to San Saba, Texas, and again affiliated himself with a local church. He worked on a ranch and raced horses. It was there he fell in with another infamous murderer, Emmanuel Clements. After Ballinger City Marshal Joe Townsend killed Clements in a gunfight, Miller ambushed the lawman. Using a shotgun, he blasted off the marshall's right arm. Townsend survived, and Miller fled to New Mexico.

In 1891, he moved on, this time to Pecos, Texas. Again, he quickly became known as an upstanding member of the church. Walking the streets wearing a black broadcloth coat, a black hat, and black boots, Miller looked more like a Puritan than an assassin. It was in Pecos that he earned the tag "Deacon Jim." He married, and even became a deputy marshal.

His time as a lawman was brief. After killing several men in Pecos, under the auspices of enforcing the law, he was fired by Sheriff George A. "Bud" Frazer. In the next election, Miller ran against his old boss and lost. One day while Frazer was sitting at a table in a saloon, Miller opened the door and blew the sheriff's head off with his trusty shotgun. At his trial, Miller brought in dozens of church members to testify to his character. With a high-priced lawyer and the church's support, Deacon Jim strutted away with another acquittal.

He quickly left town and ended up in Fort Worth, where he once again established himself as a staunch member of the church. He didn't work but always seemed to have plenty of money. What townspeople didn't know was that he'd sold his soul to the devil, having been hired by cattlemen to kill herders whose sheep were destroying their grazing land. It is thought that he murdered more than a dozen men for $150 a head. Almost all of his victims were shot in the back.

Miller cared for his gun as a mother would her child. He kept it oiled and polished, and kept it broken down except when in use. The assassin carried the gun in a folded oilskin.

In 1904, he murdered James Jarrott, a lawyer who had been highly successful in representing the sheepherders in legal battles with local ranchers. He got $500 for that killing. Again, he was acquitted at trial.

After still another murder and acquittal, Deacon Jim was implicated in the murder of former Sheriff Pat Garrett. But another man was charged, so Miller went free.

Next Miller was paid $1,800 to kill U.S. Marshal Ben Collins in Orr, Oklahoma Territory. His usual shotgun ambush did the trick. By now, the public was outraged. Had he been tried in Orr, it's doubtful he could have found one man who would have voted "not guilty" when he came to trial. He was smart enough to realize what he was up against, though. Miller quietly made bail, then jumped on his horse and galloped out of town.

In 1908, the assassin turned up in Ada, Oklahoma.

On a cold winter night, Allen Augustus "Gus" Bobbitt, a retired U.S. marshall, was driving his buggy home from town. When he stopped at his gate, a shotgun blast knocked him from his seat. A second shot slammed into him, but he was still alive when a neighbor arrived and took him home. Bobbitt had seen his attacker. He told his wife that it was the well-known paid killer, Deacon Jim Miller. In fact, before he died, he wrote a stipulation in his will that gave money to law enforcement officials to hunt down Jim Miller.

Bobbitt's death was the result of a feud between him and two notorious "Indian skinners." Joe C. Allen and Jesse West owned a local saloon. It was their habit to ply Indians with liquor, get them drunk, then pay them twenty-five dollars for the 160 acres they'd received from the U.S. government. (This practice became so widespread that a law was passed making it illegal for a buyer to purchase Indian land unless approved by a federal judge.)

Once West and Allen obtained the land, it would be sold to white settlers for a huge profit. They became so wealthy that they were able to purchase the Corner Saloon. But Bobbitt's crusade against them caused the unscrupulous pair to flee to Texas. It was there, through an intermediary named D. B. Burwell, that they paid Deacon Jim $2,000 to kill Bobbitt.

But Miller made a couple of fatal mistakes. He let Bobbitt see his face and live long enough to identify him. And, while fleeing the scene, he dropped his wire cutters and the oil cloth he used to wrap his shotgun.

He was quickly arrested, along with his co-conspirators, Allen, West, and Burwell.

By now, the citizens of Ada were fed up. When Miller hired an attorney with a 90 percent success rate in defending accused murderers, he sealed his fate.

On the evening of April 19, 1909, a group of citizens overpowered jail guards, dragged the four men to an abandoned livestock barn, and strung them up. The vigilantes left three other accused murderers unmolested in their cells. Although the governor expressed outrage at the lynching, there was little investigation into the crime, and no one was ever charged. In fact, one local publication took the position that the lynching was justified in the sight of both man and God.

What made these presumably law-abiding citizens take the law into their own hands?

Let's examine Ada, Oklahoma. In 1909, the town had a population of about 5,000 people. Until recently, it had been known as the murder capital of Oklahoma. Violent crime was so rampant that at least one saloon had a cemetery behind it. The area surrounding the saloon was nicknamed "the bloody bucket" by locals.

But by 1909, the town had cleaned itself up. Gus Bobbitt had taken the lead in helping rid the town of undesirables. Times were changing. Schools brought educators into the community. Churches brought ministers. Businesses brought, if not prosperity, at least convenience for shoppers. A newspaper recorded events and appealed to the consciences of townspeople.

So the slaying of a decent, honest man who had worked to improve his community was like turning the clock back to those years of lawlessness. Then, when the murderer Miller hired an expert defense attorney known for obtaining acquittals, citizens could envision him walking free again.

Order—that fragile bulb surrounding civilized society—was cracking. This, the citizens of Ada decided, could not be allowed to happen.

In that context, it is understandable why they lynched Deacon Jim and his cohorts.

But why would residents of dozens of other towns fight back when bank robbers entered their communities? After all, weren't bankers the enemy of the common man? Weren't these greedy usurers the very group folk-singer Woody Guthrie was referring to when he wrote that "some folks'll rob you with a six-gun, others with a fountain pen?"

Even though many people distrusted banks in general and resented the "usury" (e.g., interest) charged, as well as the threat of foreclosure, bankers were their neighbors. They shopped together, attended church together, socialized, and were friends. Banks employed their sons and daughters and husbands and wives. Banks were the depository of their money and other valuables. And, even though the banks were insured, there was something cowardly about letting a gang of thieves prance into a community and walk away with something they never earned.

Call it indignation. Or town pride. Or provincialism.

Experienced outlaws recognized the dangers of armed townspeople and tried to make allowances. In all but a few towns, many (if not most) men carried guns. Almost all men were hunters. Many had served in the military. They believed that self-defense was a God-given right, much as life, liberty, and the pursuit of happiness was a right. Most businesses kept guns on the premises in case of a robbery.

Robbers, knowing this, almost always stationed at least one armed guard outside as a lookout. His job was to discourage resistance. At the first sign of trouble, the lookout was to spray bullets toward those who became too curious. This, the bandits hoped, would discourage vigilantes.

But as we have seen, all of their best-laid plans often didn't work. Numerous robbers died or were captured as a result of gun battles with armed citizens.

What about monetary rewards as a motivation to fight back? Banker's associations were quick to offer such rewards but were reluctant to actually pay out the cash. Few citizens ever collected anything except accolades from bankers. Still, it must have gone through the minds of many.

In the end, it often boiled down to townspeople reacting to what they considered a threat to their community.

Many an outlaw learned too late that people defending their homes are among the most dangerous people to cross. Graveyards throughout the American frontier are filled with thugs who learned that lesson too late.

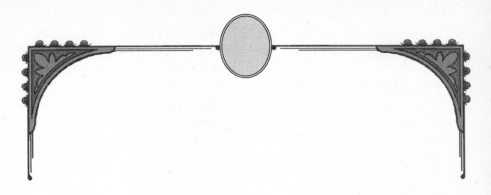

Bibliography

BOOKS

Balousek, Marv. *More Wisconsin Crimes of the Century*. Waubesa Press, 1993.

Brant, Marley. *Jesse James: The Man and the Myth*. Berkeley Publishing Group, 1998.

Elliott, David Stewart. *Last Raid of the Daltons and Battle with the Bandits at Coffeyville, Kansas*—Oct. 5, 1892. Reprint of 1892 booklet published by the editor of the *Coffeyville Journal*.

Green, A. C. *The Santa Claus Bank Robbery*. (Revised Edition.) University of North Texas Press, September 1999.

Helmer, William with Mattix, Rick. *Public Enemies: America's Criminal Past 1919-1940*. Check Mark Books, An Imprint of Facts on File, 1998.

King, Jeffery S. *The Life and Death of Pretty Boy Floyd*. The Kent State University Press, Kent, Ohio, 1998.

Koblas, John. *The Jesse James Northfield Raid: Confessions of the Ninth Man*. North Star Press of St. Cloud Inc., St. Cloud, Minnesota, 1999.

Lynch, Larry and Russell, John, Editors. *Where the Wild Rice Grows*. Dunn County Historical Society, Menomonie, Wisconsin, 1996.

McMurtry, Larry and Diana Osana. *Pretty Boy Floyd: A Novel*. Simon & Schuster, New York, 1994.

Moulton, Candy. *The Writer's Guide to Everyday Life in the Wild West from 1840-1900*. Writer's Digest Books, 1999.

Nash, Jay Robert. *Encyclopedia of Western Lawmen and Outlaws*. DeCapo Press, 1994.

Robinson, Charles M. III. *The Men Who Wear the Star: The Story of the Texas Rangers*. Random House, New York, 2000.

Schoenberger, Dale T. *The Gunfighters*. The Caxton Printers Ltd., Caldwell, Idaho, 1983.

Shirley, Glenn. *Henry Starr: Last of the Real Bad Men*. David McKay Company Inc., New York, 1965.

Sifakis, Carl. *The Encyclopedia of American Crime*, Second Edition, Vol. II. Facts on File, 2001.

Smith, Robert Barr. *Daltons! The Raid on Coffeyville, Kansas*. University of Oklahoma Press, Norman, Oklahoma, 1999.

Smith, Robert Barr. *The Last Hurrah of the James-Younger Gang*. University of Oklahoma Press, Norman, Oklahoma, 2001.

Soule, Arthur. *The Tall Texan: The Story of Ben Kilpatrick*. Self-published, 1997.

Udall, Stewart L. and Emmons, David. *The Forgotten Founders: Rethinking the History of the Old West*. Island Press, 2002.

PERIODICALS AND PAMPHLETS

Curtis, Olga. "The Bank Robbers Who Became Tourist Attractions." *Empire Magazine*, July 25, 1976.

Dirst, Shelley and Rose, Sammie. "Banker Shot Starr in Harrison." *Boone County Historian*, Vol. XIX, No. IIII.

Dirst, Shelley and Rose, Sammie. "The Outlaw, Henry Starr." *Boone County Historian*. Vol. XX, No. I.

McMahan, Hazel Ruby (Ed.) "Stories of Early Oklahoma—A collection of interesting facts, biographical sketches and stories relating to the settlement of Oklahoma": Boley. Oklahoma Historical Society.

McRae, Bennie J. Jr. *Attempted Bank Robbery in Boley, Oklahoma*. LWF Publications, Trotwood, Ohio, 1997.

McRae, Bennie J., Jr. *Hillard Taylor—The Man Who Has Cotton "On His Brain."* LWF Publications, no date.

Titsworth, B. D. "Hole in the Wall Gang." *True West*, December 1956.

Titsworth, B. D. "Hole in the Wall Gang." *True West*, February 1957.

Veselenak, Aaron J. Arthur J. Tuttle: "Dean of the Federal Bench." The Historical Society of the United States District Court for the Eastern District of Michigan, 1998.

Veselenak, Aaron J. "Making Legal History—The Execution of Anthony Chebatoris." The Historical Society of the United States District Court for the Eastern District of Michigan. Vol. VI, No. 2, Fall 1998.

NEWSPAPERS

The Daily Ardmoreite. April 19, 1909.

The Oklahoma Leader. Jan. 21 and 28, 1914; Jan. 23, Feb. 4, March 4, April 1, April 8, and April 15, 1915.

The Stroud (Okla.) Democrat. April 2, 1915; May 10, 1918.

Lincoln County News. May 6, May 13, May 20, and May 27, 1982; Jan. 12, 1984.

The Harrison (Ark.) Times. Feb. 19, 1921.

Harrison (Ark.) Daily Times. Sept. 17, 1974.

The Daily Oklahoman. Feb. 24, Feb. 28, March 10, March 11, Nov. 26, and Nov. 28, 1932; April 5, 1959.

The Dunn County News. Oct. 22, 1931.

The Saginaw (Mich.) News. (No Date—Article Summarizes story of Anthony Chebatoris.)

Sulphur (Okla.) Times-Democrat. March 17, 1932.

Johnston County Capital Democrat. March 10 and March 17, 1932.

Lincoln County News. May 13 and May 27, 1982; June 12, 1984.

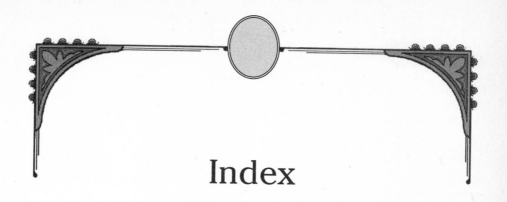

Index